Quiet-Time
Prayers
for a
Girl's Heart

180 Comforting
Conversations with God

HILARY
BERNSTEIN

BARBOUR **kidz**
A Division of Barbour Publishing

Published by Barbour Publishing, Inc., 1810 Barbour Drive, Uhrichsville, Ohio 44683, www.barbourbooks.com

Member of the
Evangelical Christian
Publishers Association

Our mission is to inspire the world with the life-changing message of the Bible.

Printed in the United States of America.

001225 0622 SP

Quiet-Time
Prayers
for a
Girl's Heart

A Little Quiet Time Is GOOD for Your Heart, Girl!

No matter where you are right now, you're not alone. God is with you! He sees you, He hears you, and He knows you. Before He created this earth, He knew He would create you in His image. He even knew you needed to live right here and right now. Even though God knows (and loves!) everything about you, you may not feel like you know that much about Him. The good news is He doesn't stay secretive, leaving you to guess what He must be like. You can learn all about Him in the Bible. When you do spend time alone with Him by reading the Bible, thinking over what you've read, and praying, you'll get to know Him more and more. You'll discover His Word has a lot to say that helps make your life better too! As you spend quiet time with your heavenly Father, enjoy the comfort only He can bring!

Come to Me

"Come to Me, all of you who work and have heavy loads. I will give you rest. Follow My teachings and learn from Me. I am gentle and do not have pride. You will have rest for your souls."

MATTHEW 11:28–29

Lord, knowing that You invite me to come to You is such a relief. I don't need to pretend I'm someone I'm not. I can forget about being perfect. I can come to You, just as I am, imperfect and confused. I can bring You all my worries and doubts, and You'll gladly take them from me. Sometimes I feel so weighed down by all that's buzzing around my mind. But when I come to You and tell You all my worries, You give me Your peace. From the inside out, You make me strong to keep going. Thank You!

GROWING IN WISDOM

*For wisdom is better than stones
of great worth. All that you may
desire cannot compare with her.*

PROVERBS 8:11

Father, a lot of things in this world compete for my attention. It's easy to get caught up in focusing on things or friends or how well I'm doing at school. But when I think about You and what the Bible says, I don't have to worry about those things. What I really need is wisdom! Could You please help me get wiser? Proverbs promises that wisdom is better than fancy jewels. I have a problem though. I don't know how to be wise on my own. But You're wise! Could You please share some of Your wisdom with me? I'd love to have Your kind of understanding about life. I'd be lost without You! In Jesus' name I pray, amen.

At Peace

*Now that we have been made right
with God by putting our trust in Him,
we have peace with Him. It is because
of what our Lord Jesus Christ did for us.*

ROMANS 5:1

Lord, more than anything else, I want to be made right with You! I don't want to be wrong in Your eyes. I love You and want to give my life to You! No one else. To do that, I need to trust You completely. And I do! I put my trust in Jesus. Totally trusting Him seems like a big task, because I give absolutely everything to Him. But it's actually pretty simple too. I don't have to worry about working hard to make peace with You on my own, because it's all through Jesus. Thank You for the way Jesus makes me right with You! I love You.

WHO AM I?

When I look up and think about Your heavens, the work of Your fingers, the moon and the stars, which You have set in their place, what is man, that You think of him, the son of man that You care for him?

PSALM 8:3–4

Lord, You're amazing! You've created absolutely everything, from wonders like the ocean and mountains and the starry night sky, to teensy tiny miracles like insects and seeds and cells in my body. What You've done is way more than I can ever understand. You are so great, and I worship You. Thank You that out of all creation, You chose to make humans in Your own image and care for us too. Thank You for Your kindness! You're so very good to me. I don't even want to imagine what life would be like without Your good gifts. Thank You!

Gathered and Carried

He will feed His flock like a shepherd. He will gather the lambs in His arms and carry them close to His heart. He will be gentle in leading those that are with young.

ISAIAH 40:11

Father, sometimes I feel a little lost in this world. Knowing You'll take care of everything I need and carry me close to Your heart is such a huge relief and comfort. When I try to do everything on my own and make my own big decisions, it's hard! It's confusing to know what's a right or wrong choice. It feels too hard to make and rely on my decisions. But You're just like a good shepherd. You know where I'm headed, and You want to keep me close by Your side, like a sweet little lamb. Please lead me through life in a clear way. I want to listen to You. I love You!

A LIGHT WILL SHINE

"Because the heart of our God is full of loving-kindness for us, a light from heaven will shine on us. It will give light to those who live in darkness and are under the shadow of death. It will lead our feet in the way of peace."

LUKE 1:78–79

Father, when I watch the sun rise in the morning, I'm amazed. As the Master Artist, You paint the sky in such pretty colors. What's amazing is the way sunrises show me so much about what will come someday. This world is a dark place without Jesus. Without Him, people stumble in darkness. It's no wonder it feels like there's so much evil and confusion! But Jesus is the light. He visited earth to rescue people and offer them life that lasts forever. Thank You for sending Him! Thank You for the way He lights my world! Amen.

No Worries

*"He will be like a tree planted by the water,
that sends out its roots by the river. It will
not be afraid when the heat comes but its
leaves will be green. It will not be troubled
in a dry year, or stop giving fruit."*

JEREMIAH 17:8

Lord, when I look around at all that's happening in the world, it's easy to feel worried. But when I stick close to You, I don't have to be discouraged by the world's troubles. I don't have to worry. Instead, when I trust in You, I can be like a tree planted by streams of water. You'll keep me blooming and growing, even when it seems like everything around me is shriveled and dry. When I stay rooted in You with prayer and Bible reading, good things will come in my life. Thank You!

Paying Attention

*I am sure that God Who began the good
work in you will keep on working in you
until the day Jesus Christ comes again.*

PHILIPPIANS 1:6

Father, it's amazing to know that You've started a
good work in me. You've even planned how You'll
work in my life. Who am I to deserve all Your love
and kindness and attention? Sometimes I can
see moments when You're doing really great
things for me. It's so exciting! And other times, I
feel like I get in Your way. Please help me trust
You more and more each day. Sometimes it
seems like I need You to use a megaphone! I
want to carefully listen for Your voice and Your
direction. I know I can trust You! Amen.

Strength and Peace

The Lord will give strength to His people.
The Lord will give His people peace.

PSALM 29:11

Lord, thank You for Your really good gifts! You know me better than I know myself, and You know I don't always feel very strong. You have an amazing way of taking my fears away and giving me Your peace. Instead of worrying about what might happen, I want to think about You. When I think about You instead of what is going on around me, everything changes. You offer me peace. You can change my weakness into strength when I depend on You. I want to stop trying to do things on my own and rely on You instead. You deserve my trust! In Jesus' name I pray, amen.

Don't Give Up

*"But you be strong. Do not
lose strength of heart."*
2 CHRONICLES 15:7

Father, it's so tempting to give up! When I feel challenged—whether people give me a hard time or things just seem too difficult—it's hard to keep going. I don't always feel like fighting through hard times. But I need to remember that it's really good to keep going. Sticking with things feels so hard, but it's what's best. As I wait and try to keep going, could You help me? Please give me strength so I don't give up. I may not feel like I'm strong enough to do everything right now, but with You and Your help, I can do the next right thing. Thank You for never leaving me on my own. I love You! In Jesus' name I pray, amen.

Lots of Love

Our Lord Jesus Christ and God our Father loves us. Through His loving-favor He gives us comfort and hope that lasts forever. May He give your hearts comfort and strength to say and do every good thing.

2 THESSALONIANS 2:16–17

Lord Jesus, You've given me so many wonderful things. Thank You! With Your great love, You've comforted me. You've given me hope that lasts forever. You make my heart feel good in a way that nothing or no one else can. And You fill me with Your strength so I can say and do good things. Apart from You, I could try to find comfort, hope, and strength. I could try to say and do every good thing on my own. But You and I both know I wouldn't get very far! I really need Your help, and I'm thankful for the ways You fill my life with Your goodness. Amen.

THere IS HOPe!

"If you set your heart right, and put out your hands to Him. . . Your life would be brighter than noon. Darkness would be like the morning. Then you would trust, because there is hope. You would look around and rest and be safe."

JOB 11:13, 17–18

Father, when I try to do things on my own, things don't always make sense. Sometimes I feel like I'm wandering around in the dark instead of in Your brightness. But it doesn't have to be that way! Instead of relying on myself, I can turn to You. So many good things come when I trust You! You brighten my life and clearly show me Your way. You keep me safe, so I can relax and rest in You. Please lead and guide me in Your way. In Jesus' name I pray, amen.

No Confusion

God does not want everyone speaking at the same time in church meetings. He wants peace.
1 CORINTHIANS 14:33

Lord God, You are not a God of confusion! You brought chaos into order during Creation. You have a clear plan and direction for everyone. When I turn to You, You'll fill me with Your peace. This is such a great gift! I hate the way I feel when I'm confused. It never seems right to feel mixed up and out of sorts. I don't like having scattered thoughts. To know that You never experience any of that confusion is amazing. You are a God of order and peace. You make things clear. What a relief! You are so awesome and amazing. I worship You!

Waiting in Hope

Our soul waits for the Lord. He is our help and our safe cover. For our heart is full of joy in Him, because we trust in His holy name. O Lord, let Your loving-kindness be upon us as we put our hope in You.
PSALM 33:20–22

Lord, waiting is really hard for me to do. I get frustrated and impatient. I want things to happen right away. It's hard to wait and see what You'll do or how You'll answer my prayers. But You're my help. You're my protector. You love me so faithfully. When I do put my hope and trust in You, I can wait for You to work out Your perfect plans. I don't have to rush ahead and try to make things happen. Instead, I want to wait for You. I want to hope in You and You alone. In Jesus' name I pray, amen.

Do Not Fear

But now the Lord Who made you, O Jacob, and He Who made you, O Israel, says, "Do not be afraid. For I have bought you and made you free. I have called you by name. You are Mine! When you pass through the waters, I will be with you. When you pass through the rivers, they will not flow over you. When you walk through the fire, you will not be burned. The fire will not destroy you. For I am the Lord your God, the Holy One of Israel, Who saves you."

ISAIAH 43:1–3

Lord, it's amazing to know that because of the way You love me, I don't have to be afraid! In the Bible, You reminded Israel that You called them and cared for them in amazing ways time and time again. They were Your chosen people. In my own life, You've created me. And through Jesus, You've also chosen me. You're with me, no matter what. You'll care for me in amazing ways too. Thank You!

LiSTeN!

*"The Holy Spirit is coming. He will lead
you into all truth. He will not speak His
Own words. He will speak what He hears.
He will tell you of things to come."*

JOHN 16:13

Father, when Jesus was on earth, He promised the Holy Spirit would come to believers. Just like Jesus promised, Your Holy Spirit did come! When I believe all that Jesus said and did, Your Holy Spirit is part of me. He leads me in a gentle but mighty way. Please help me pay attention to Him! I want to obey Him. As He speaks what He hears from You, please help me hear and understand. I want to trust that His leading is right. I want to do Your will, even if I need to boldly step out in faith. I love You!

Rest

*"Remember what the Lord's servant Moses
told you, saying, 'The Lord your God gives
you rest, and will give you this land.'"*
JOSHUA 1:13

Lord, rest is a great thing. I love to take it easy and relax! You created everything in six days, but You rested on the seventh day. You didn't need to rest—You're God!—but You knew humans would need rest. You give rest in an amazing and refreshing way. Jesus also promised, "Come to Me, all of you who work and have heavy loads. I will give you rest" (Matthew 11:28). I don't have to be so concerned about doing so much and working way too hard until I'm exhausted. I can trust that You'll do what You need to do through me. I don't know how You work through me, but I know You do. I want to stop worrying and trust You completely. Please help me find my rest in You. Amen.

THE ANCHOR OF MY SOUL

This hope is a safe anchor for our souls. It will never move. This hope goes into the Holiest Place of All behind the curtain of heaven.

HEBREWS 6:19

Father, I don't always feel sure of what I'm thinking or feeling. Sometimes all of life's uncertainty leaves me feeling really scared and worried. But I don't need to feel like a toy boat being tossed around in a stormy ocean. I'm actually safe and secure because of Jesus. When I put all my hope and trust in Him, He becomes the anchor of my soul. He keeps me firmly in place, even in the rockiest, stormiest moments of life. I might feel the waves, but I won't be wrecked or ruined. In moments when I feel scared, please remind me of my soul's anchor. In Jesus' name I pray, amen.

Lifting My Head

*But You, O Lord, are a covering
around me, my shining-greatness,
and the One Who lifts my head.*

PSALM 3:3

Lord, when I'm afraid or start worrying, it's easy to look down. Either I try to mind my own business, or I just don't want to see people looking at me. It crushes me when someone else makes fun of me or bullies me. But You're my protector. In fact, You protect me like a shield! I don't have to worry about myself. I don't have to worry about what I look like or how well I do things, because You're the One at work. When I trust You completely, You'll shine through me. I don't have to look down in shame, because You're the One who lifts my head high. In You, I can be completely confident. Thank You for Your never-ending protection. Amen.

Going Before Me

The Lord went before them, in a pillar of cloud during the day to lead them on the way, and in a pillar of fire during the night to give them light. So they could travel day and night.

EXODUS 13:21

Lord, when You faithfully led the Israelites through the desert for forty years, You never, ever failed them. In fact, You led them all the time—by cloud during the daytime and by fire during the night. Please help me remember that You'll lead me too. Even if I'd like Your guidance to be as obvious as fire or a cloud, please help me pay attention to what You'd like me to do. You go before me to get things ready ahead of time. That's pretty amazing, and I'm so thankful for that. I want to look for You more and more every day. In Jesus' name I pray, amen.

SHOWING RESPECT

First of all, I ask you to pray much for all men and to give thanks for them. Pray for kings and all others who are in power over us so we might live quiet God-like lives in peace.
1 TIMOTHY 2:1–2

Father, I don't always like someone else telling me what to do, even if I know it's for my own good. Please help me realize that You're the One who puts leaders in place. You've chosen who will rule and guide. Whether I agree with my leaders or not, please help me respect them with my attitude and the way I act. Help me re-member to pray for them, that they might lead well and make wise decisions. Please help me be a good follower of people who are in power over me. When I'm tempted to disobey, help me make a peaceful, respectful choice that reflects my love for You. Amen.

KEPT AND HIDDEN

Keep me safe as You would Your own eye.
Hide me in the shadow of Your wings, from
the sinful who fight against me, those who
would kill me and are all around me.

PSALM 17:8–9

Father, I don't know why some people don't like me, but it's obvious they don't. And it hurts. Please show me if I've sinned against these people or if I'm innocent and free from blame. Please show me if I need to change something in my own life. I don't want to try to solve things on my own. Instead, I want to run to You. Please hide me in the shadow of Your wings. And keep me as the apple of Your eye. I know You love me and want what's best for me. Even when it seems tough, I want to become more and more like You. Amen.

MULTiPLieD GOODNeSS

I am writing to you who have been chosen by God the Father. You are kept for Jesus Christ. May you have much of God's loving-kindness and peace and love.
JUDE 1:1–2

Lord, when I think of all the goodness You offer me, I'm really amazed. You give me so much more than I deserve! You've chosen me. You're kind and forgiving. You love me so much, and Your love always keeps going. Even if I don't feel like I deserve all of this, You're happy to multiply Your mercy, peace, and love just for me. I want to think about all the good You have for me instead of focusing on bad things that happen in my day. Please help me be like a detective and search out Your wonderful gifts so I can thank You for them. Amen.

MY HiDinG PLace

*You are my hiding place. You keep me
safe from trouble. All around me are
your songs of being made free.*

PSALM 32:7

Father, some days I'd like to curl up into a tiny
ball and escape from real life. Sometimes I'm in
the middle of a bad day when everything seems
to be going wrong, and other times I imagine
all sorts of troubles and bad things that could
happen in the future. The amazing thing I need
to remember, though, is that You're my hiding place. You'll protect me from trouble. You'll
rescue me. Even on my worst days, I can put
all my trust in You, because I know You'll work
all the details out for my good. Even if I feel
helpless or hopeless, there's *always* hope with
You. In Jesus' name I pray, amen.

He'll Never Get Tired

Have you not known? Have you not heard?
The God Who lives forever is the Lord, the
One Who made the ends of the earth. He will
not become weak or tired. His understanding
is too great for us to begin to know. He
gives strength to the weak. And He gives
power to him who has little strength.
ISAIAH 40:28–29

Creator God, You are awesome! When I think about how tired I can get, it's amazing to realize You never, ever get tired. Absolutely nothing wears You out. You created all things, and You hold everything together. When I do get tired, You'll give me strength. When I feel weak and small, You'll increase my power in amazing ways. Because of You, I'll always have strength. I worship You for the amazing God You are! In Jesus' name I pray, amen.

Hope to Honor

I hope very much that I will have no reason to be ashamed. I hope to honor Christ with my body if it be by my life or by my death. I want to honor Him without fear, now and always.

PHILIPPIANS 1:20

Jesus, You've done so very much for me! You left Your home in heaven to come to earth, live a life without any sin, and then die on the cross. You came back to life three days later, showed Yourself to lots of people, and then You went back to heaven. You chose me to believe in You. Once I say I believe in You, I can spend forever with You. Because of all Your great gifts for me, I want the things I say and do and think to show how much I adore You. In Your name I pray, amen.

PLEASING TO THE LORD

*The religious leader said to them,
"Go in peace. The way you are
going is pleasing to the Lord."*

JUDGES 18:6

Lord, I love You. I'm so thankful You're my God. Please help me say and do things that please You. When I make decisions every day, please show me what choices will point to the fact that I'm Your daughter. As I follow You, please fill me with Your Spirit and help me live out Your love, joy, and peace. Please help me be patient with others. I want to grow to become a kind girl who is good, faithful, and gentle. Please help me live a life of self-control. I could try all of this on my own and only get frustrated with my failures and sins. But if You're working through me, I know You can do anything. In Your name I pray, amen.

Choosing a Friendship

Do you not know that to love the sinful things of the world and to be a friend to them is to be against God? Yes, I say it again, if you are a friend of the world, you are against God.
JAMES 4:4

Father, temptation is so powerful! You know this, because humans have been dealing with it ever since Eve was tempted in the Garden of Eden. No matter how inviting my temptations might feel, when I choose to sin it really means I choose against You. Am I devoted to You? Do I really love You? If I do, I want and need to choose You. If I'm not loyal to You, I'll cave in to the world's pressures and pleasures. I don't want to be a friend of the world. Please help me see the sinful thoughts and choices so I can run from them. I want to be Your friend! Amen.

IN Pursuit of Peace

*Turn away from what is sinful. Do what
is good. Look for peace and follow it.*

PSALM 34:14

Father, I know the good things I do won't save me. Only Jesus can do that. But I do pray that I'll be good and do good things. In fact, I want to be known for my kindness and for the way I help make other people's days better. When I'm tempted to react in frustration or anger or revenge, please stop me in my tracks. Help me recognize and turn away from bad things. Even when people are mean or hurt my feelings, help me try to make peace with them. This isn't easy. But with You and Your help, I can do hard things. Please help me be good and give me peace! In Jesus' name I pray, amen.

Success

*And from the time that he watched over his
house and all he owned, the Lord brought
good to the Egyptian's house because of
Joseph. The Lord brought good upon all
that he owned in the house and in the field.
So he put all he owned in Joseph's care.
Having Joseph near, he did not need to
think about anything but the food he ate.*
GENESIS 39:5–6

Lord, I'm glad You've included stories of real
men and women in the Bible. I can relate to
the way their lives had twists and turns. Not
everything goes perfectly and smoothly. Thank
You for working in Joseph's life in an amazing
way. You had a perfect plan for him, even when
he found himself in absolutely awful situations.
Even as a prisoner, Joseph became a success.
Could You please look on me with Your favor?
Would You please help me succeed in the things
I do? Amen.

COMFORTED

We give thanks to the God and Father of our Lord Jesus Christ. He is our Father Who shows us loving-kindness and our God Who gives us comfort. He gives us comfort in all our troubles. Then we can comfort other people who have the same troubles. We give the same kind of comfort God gives us.

2 CORINTHIANS 1:3–4

God, I praise You because You're good. You created a beautiful world where we live. I praise You! You created all people, and You know everyone completely. I praise You! You didn't just create me, but You're filled with loving-kindness for me too. Thank You! You comfort me whenever I'm feeling down or when trouble comes my way. You never stop caring for me. Your concern for me never stops, whether I realize it or not. Please help me use Your comfort to help others. Amen.

HeLP Me!

I called to the Lord in my trouble. I cried to God for help. He heard my voice from His holy house. My cry for help came into His ears.

PSALM 18:6

Lord God, help! I feel so helpless and alone right now. It seems like everything is out of my control, and I don't know what will happen. Even if I don't know what's going on, You do. Even if I'm out of control, You're in complete control. Thank You that I can tell You every single detail of what's going on, no matter how big or small it might seem. As I cry and pray and beg You for help, You hear and know and will answer. I trust You completely. Please fill me with Your peace as I wait to see the amazing ways You'll help me. Amen.

Stop Worrying

"I tell you this: Do not worry about your life. Do not worry about what you are going to eat and drink. Do not worry about what you are going to wear. Is not life more important than food? Is not the body more important than clothes?"
MATTHEW 6:25

Oh Father, it's easy to worry about a lot of things. I can obsess over every little detail, whether it involves my family or friends or school or my future. Lots of other little details are easy to worry about too. Please help me remember Your big picture though. My life is more than the food I eat—and boy, do I like my favorite foods! My life is more than the clothes I wear or what I look like. I don't have to worry about those things or anything else. I want to kiss my worries goodbye and focus on trusting You—not what might or might not happen. Amen.

GOOD THINGS

For the Lord God is a sun and a safe-covering. The Lord gives favor and honor. He holds back nothing good from those who walk in the way that is right. O Lord of all, how happy is the man who trusts in You!
PSALM 84:11–12

Lord God, You do so many amazing things for me. You protect me in ways I'll never realize. As long as I walk with You through my life and live with complete trust in You, You'll bless me with every good thing. How wonderful! When I'm tempted to get sidetracked by something or someone else, You help me to keep my eyes on You. I want to stay so close to You, because You're my sun and my shield. When I trust in You, I'm happy! You more than deserve my praise and my thanks. In Jesus' name I pray, amen.

FOLLOW THE LEADER

"I have seen his ways and will heal him.
I will lead him and give comfort to him
and to those who have sorrow for him."
ISAIAH 57:18

Father, Your love and kindness for me are amazing! When I want to follow You with my whole heart and my whole life, You lead me. I don't know what's coming, but You make every step of mine certain. You keep my path straight even when I have no idea what's coming next. Because of You, I don't have to fear. Plus, You comfort me in amazing ways. It's tempting to focus on all that I can see. I get frustrated easily, and it's hard to go through tough times. But every single day, You're with me. Please help me follow You when and where You lead me! In Jesus' name I pray, amen.

DISTRACTED

Martha was working hard getting the supper ready. She came to Jesus and said, "Do You see that my sister is not helping me? Tell her to help me." Jesus said to her, "Martha, Martha, you are worried and troubled about many things. Only a few things are important, even just one. Mary has chosen the good thing. It will not be taken away from her."
LUKE 10:40–42

Lord, it's easy for me to blame other people. It's also easy to get distracted. Whether it's school or chores or activities or spending time with my family and friends, when I focus on what I need to do, it's easy to feel stressed out. Instead of focusing so much on other people or keeping busy, please help me find time just to be with You. I want to get to know who You are through the Bible and prayer. Please help me focus on You! Amen.

LiViNg iN TruTH

"These are the things you are to do: Speak the truth to one another. Judge with truth so there will be peace within your gates."

ZECHARIAH 8:16

Father, sometimes it would be nice to know what I should or shouldn't do because it's easier to know what's expected of me. I'm thankful the Bible gives me details of what You'd like my life to look like. When I'm tempted to stretch the truth, please help me choose honesty instead. When it seems like a lie would be an easier way to cover up something that's difficult or uncomfortable to say, please help me be truthful! I need to speak the truth. Even when it's difficult and even when I'm tempted to make an easier, dishonest choice, please help me choose what's right and true. In Jesus' name I pray, amen.

THE COMPARISON TRAP

We do not compare ourselves with those who think they are good. They compare themselves with themselves. They decide what they think is good or bad and compare themselves with those ideas. They are foolish.
2 CORINTHIANS 10:12

Oh Father, it's so hard to not pay attention to what other people are doing. Sometimes I think I'm better than someone else or simply not good enough. It's like I measure myself on a scale that's constantly changing. I don't want to compare myself with others. Please help me remember that You've created every single person uniquely. We all have different strengths and weaknesses, and You have a completely different plan for every single life. I want to be happy with the life You've given me. I want to be the best me possible, and I can't do that if I'm constantly trying to copy or be better than other people. Amen.

Peace and Safety

I will lie down and sleep in peace.
O Lord, You alone keep me safe.
PSALM 4:8

Oh Lord, as much as I might try to find my security or safety in other things or people, You alone are the One who floods my heart with peace. You alone are the One who keeps me safe. Thank You! When I lie down tonight, please help me remember this. I want to give You all the cares of my day, thank You for everything good that's happened, and truly rest in You. I don't have to worry about anything that's happened in my day or anything that might happen tomorrow. Everything's under Your control. Thank You for protecting me. Thank You for Your good, comforting gift of peace! In Jesus' name I pray, amen.

A Strong Guide

*You have led with loving-kindness the
people You have made free. You have led
them in Your strength to Your holy place.*
EXODUS 15:13

Father, all throughout the Bible, You've given
examples of the ways You've taken care of
people You've chosen. In the Old Testament,
You led the Israelites in a mighty and mirac-
ulous way. And in the New Testament, You
faithfully guided and worked through people
who trusted in You completely. I'm in awe of
the way You work situations for good for those
who know and love You. I'm in awe of the way
You provide for every single need. And I'm
in awe of the way You lovingly and patiently
guide. None of this is half-hearted on Your part.
I want You to guide me too! I love You and trust
You! In Jesus' name I pray, amen.

COMPLETE REST

And so God's people have a complete
rest waiting for them. The man who goes
into God's rest, rests from his own work
the same as God rested from His work.
HEBREWS 4:9–10

Father, You created all things. You created the entire world and everything in it in six days! It was good. Then You rested. As the God of the universe, I'm sure You didn't need to rest, but You did as an example for me. Then through Your gift of Jesus, You offered me complete soul rest. When I believe in Him, I don't have to do more or try to be more. I don't have to work to try to save myself. Thank You for offering me Your good rest. I'll happily take it! I pray that as I do, I'll stop trying to work so hard for Your love and approval. Amen.

A MUCH-NEEDED RESCUE

O my God, take me away from those who hate me. Put me up high above those who rise up against me. Take me away from those who do wrong. And save me from those who kill.

PSALM 59:1–2

Lord, You know who my enemies are, even if I don't. Please rescue me! Please keep me safe from evil plans. Please protect me from people who want to harm me. Please confuse any plans of the wicked. I get so frustrated and angry when it seems like evil people do well. Please help me remember that You know exactly what people do and that You'll punish evil. When I get scared, please comfort me and remind me that You're my strong, safe place. I'm depending on You! In Your name I pray, amen.

THE RiGHT WOrDS at THE RiGHT TiME

*"When you are put into their hands,
do not worry what you will say or
how you will say it. The words will
be given you when the time comes."*

MATTHEW 10:19

Father, it's easy for me to wonder what will happen to me in my life. Will evil people rule over me? Will I be punished for my faith in You? When I have so many ideas and questions, please help me remember that You're the ultimate Answer. When I trust You completely, You'll give me the exact words to say at the right time. I don't have to worry. I don't have to plan what I'll say or do. All I need is to trust You. I love You and want to rest in the peace that only You can bring. Thank You for being completely deserving of my trust. I love You!

Greater THAN I Realize

I looked for the Lord, and He answered me. And He took away all my fears.

PSALM 34:4

Lord, some of the many amazing things about You are these. . .When I look for You, I'll find You. When I call to You, You'll answer me. When I'm scared, You'll take away all my fears. You're always there, always listening, and always ready to help me. You're so much greater and kinder than I realize. Unfortunately I don't always make the most of Your faithfulness and love. Some days I forget about You. I get busy and forgetful. I don't always look for You. I don't talk to You or listen for You as much as I'd like. And sometimes I'd rather think about my worries and fears instead of totally placing my trust in You. Please help me turn to You more and more every day. In Jesus' name I pray, amen.

GLaDNeSS aND JoY

"Then the young women who have never had a man will dance for joy, and the young men and old as well. For I will change their sorrow to joy, and will comfort them. I will give them joy for their sorrow."

JEREMIAH 31:13

Father, life isn't easy. You never promised it would be; but when I face hard times, it's easy to feel discouraged. In my times of frustration, I want to turn to You. When I do, You'll change my perspective. When I trust You in hard times, You'll give me comfort I could never create on my own. Just like the prophet Jeremiah promised the Israelites, You'll replace sorrow with comfort and joy. You have the power to do that, Lord. Please do this in my life! In Your name I pray, amen.

Filled to Overflowing

*But the fruit that comes from having
the Holy Spirit in our lives is: love, joy,
peace, not giving up, being kind, being
good, having faith, being gentle, and
being the boss over our own desires.
The Law is not against these things.*
GALATIANS 5:22–23

Lord God, when I come to know You, You fill me
with Your Spirit. When He's part of my life, He
can't help but spill out of me in a wonderful way.
It's like I start producing all of this really good
fruit I could never create on my own. Through
Your Spirit, You give me true love and joy that
overflows to others. Your peace comforts me in
an amazing way. I grow in patience, both with
myself and with others. You help me be kind and
gentle with other people. Because of You, I can
be faithful and good. And You help me control
myself. Thank You!

THe Offer of Peace

"You will keep the man in perfect
peace whose mind is kept on
You, because he trusts in You."

ISAIAH 26:3

Father God, Your peace is something I can't really understand, but I definitely can experience it! And when I do, I'm amazed. I don't have to fear anything in this life. I don't have to worry. Even though You're more than willing to give me Your peace, it doesn't just come to me automatically. I have to trust in You. And I have to keep my mind on You. When I trust in myself and keep my mind focused on my own thoughts, any peace disappears and my worries start multiplying. But when I focus on You, You fill me with Your unmistakable, unshakable peace. Please help me think of You and trust in You, even when this world tries to pull my thoughts away. Amen.

DOING WHAT YOU'D LIKE

"Do not say what is wrong in other people's lives. Then other people will not say what is wrong in your life. Do not say someone is guilty. Then other people will not say you are guilty. Forgive other people and other people will forgive you."

LUKE 6:37

Lord, it's not easy to treat people the way I'd like to be treated. Please help me remember to do this though! When I'm tempted to look at what someone else is saying or doing and judge them, I want to stop. I don't want people to judge me, so I shouldn't judge them either. When I'm tempted to hold on to a grudge and be unforgiving, please help me to forgive. When I mess up or hurt someone else, I want to be forgiven. In the same way, help me forgive others too. Amen.

DON'T TURN BACK

I will listen to what God the Lord will say.
For He will speak peace to His people, to
those who are right with Him. But do not
let them turn again to foolish things.
PSALM 85:8

Lord, thank You for the way You speak peace to Your people. Because You're the Lord of the universe, You could say absolutely anything to anyone. Yet You choose Your own people, and You choose to speak peace in such a loving and gentle way. If You've called me to Yourself and I've said yes to You, I don't want to turn back to foolishness! I want to please You in all that I say and do. When I mess up and forget that I'm Your daughter, please forgive me. Then help me turn back to say and do what's right in Your sight. I love You, and I'm thankful for all You've done for me.

Pointing Others to Jesus

"Kindness from a friend should be shown to a man without hope, or he might turn away from the fear of the All-powerful."

JOB 6:14

Almighty God, the way I treat other people reflects my love and respect for You. I could treat others absolutely any way I feel like treating them. I could be mean and nasty. I could ignore them. Or, I could be caring and concerned. I could be gentle and try to make peace. I could be kind and loving. If I choose to treat others with the sort of love and kindness You've shown me, I show the world that I respect You. I can point others to Jesus by the way I treat them. Please help me remember and live this way! In Jesus' name I pray, amen.

True Beauty

Your beauty should come from the inside. It should come from the heart. This is the kind that lasts. Your beauty should be a gentle and quiet spirit. In God's sight this is of great worth and no amount of money can buy it.

1 PETER 3:4

Heavenly Father, so very much in this world focuses on outward appearances. It's hard to not get sucked in to the temptation to focus on what other people look like—or what I look like. But it doesn't matter what people look like! Please help me look beyond the outside to see who people really are. And please help me focus on making my own personality beautiful. You know my heart, and You know if it's beautiful or not. Open my eyes to see a true picture of my character, and help my spirit become beautiful. Please give my heart a makeover! Amen.

Worthy of Praise

*I call to the Lord, Who has the right
to be praised. And I am saved
from those who hate me.*
PSALM 18:3

Lord, I praise You! You are so much more amazing than I realize. You created everything! You have a plan for every single person. You notice every single detail. Nothing comes as a surprise to You. You know me completely, and You still love me. Thank You! You listen to me when I call out to You. When my enemies try to harm me or create bad situations in my life, You save me. Because of You and Your protection and care, I don't have to fear. You're worthy of my trust, and You're worthy of my praise. You're a good, good God, and I'm so thankful You've called me to be part of Your family. In Jesus' name I pray, amen.

WHaT'S RULiNg your Heart?

*Let the peace of Christ have power over
your hearts. You were chosen as a part
of His body. Always be thankful.*
COLOSSIANS 3:15

Lord God, every day I choose what will rule my
heart. Will my own feelings take control? Will
I be led by my emotions and moods? Even if I
feel like I'm just going with the flow, that's still
a decision. Open my eyes to how my thoughts
affect my attitude and actions. It's so easy to
feel like I have the right to say or do whatever
I please. Deep down, though, I know that kind
of life isn't Your best for me. When I'm tempted
to react to situations out of fear or worry, help
Jesus' peace to wash over me. Amen.

Loyalty or Lies?

They remembered that God was their rock,
and that the Most High God was the One Who
set them free. But they gave Him false honor
with their mouth. They lied to Him with their
tongue. For their heart was not right toward
Him. They were not faithful to His agreement.
PSALM 78:35–37

Oh Lord, how many times have Your chosen people worshipped You but then turned away? The Bible tells about so many people who were kind to You with their mouths but unkind to You with their hearts and choices. I don't want that to be true of me, Father! I love You! I want to be loyal to You! I don't want to change my mind. You don't need my flattery or praise. You don't want a bunch of empty words, and I don't want to be known as a liar. I want to loyally love and worship You. Amen.

Do Not Be Afraid

"Do not fear, for I am with you. Do not be afraid, for I am your God. I will give you strength, and for sure I will help you. Yes, I will hold you up with My right hand that is right and good."

ISAIAH 41:10

Father, I try to be brave on my own, but I can only do so much. You, however, can do amazing things! Because of You and Your strength and power, I don't have to fear. You're always, always with me! You're my heavenly Father, and I'm Your child. You'll protect me and help me. You'll give me strength even when I feel weak. You'll hold me up when I stumble and fall. I want to remember all the good things You do for me, so when I'm afraid or worried or nervous, I'll be comforted by You and Your truth. You're such a good, good God! Amen.

LiViNg LikE I'M CHOSEN

*God has chosen you. You are holy and
loved by Him. Because of this, your new
life should be full of loving-pity. You should
be kind to others and have no pride.
Be gentle and be willing to wait for others.*

<small>COLOSSIANS 3:12</small>

Lord, when I stop to consider that You've chosen me, I'm amazed. I didn't have to do anything for Your favor, but You've given it to me in so many ways. You love me dearly, and You even consider me to be holy. Even if I don't understand how or why I'm so special to You, I can believe it! Because I'm Yours, I want to live like it. I want what I think, say, do, and choose to reflect my love and devotion to You. I love You and want my life to mirror You. In Jesus' name I pray, amen.

Make Plans for Peace

Lying is in the heart of those who plan what
is bad, but those who plan peace have joy.
PROVERBS 12:20

Father, whether I realize it or not, all day long I make choices that reveal my heart and my intentions. I can choose wrong and try to get back at people or act out in frustration, anger, and annoyance. Or I can choose right and look for ways to make someone else's life better. Could You please help me choose what's right and do what's right in Your eyes? I don't want to plan bad things. I want to do good, even when I don't feel like it. I don't want to become a liar. I want to be honest, even when it's uncomfortable. I'd love to add peace to this world just because I'm Your daughter. In Jesus' name I pray, amen.

More THAN WHAT you See

*"Do not say a person is guilty by what
you see. Be sure you know when
you say what is right or wrong."*

JOHN 7:24

Oh Lord, so many times I judge people based
on what I see. I don't try to find out details, and I
don't stop to consider what someone else might
be going through. I need to stop doing that! You
see what's in the heart. You know what's happening behind the scenes. I'm not You, though, and
I'll never be able to have Your unlimited wisdom.
But I can try to be more like You every day. When
it comes to my thoughts and reactions toward
people, I can stop and try to get a better picture
of what might be going on. Please open my eyes
to the truth and see situations and people just
like You see them. Amen.

CHOOSING PRIDE OR HUMILITY

But those who have no pride will be given the earth. And they will be happy and have much more than they need.

PSALM 37:11

Father, so much of this world centers on pride. I can focus so much on myself and what I think is good about me until I start to get puffed up. That's not Your way though! If anyone has a reason to brag or be proud, it's You. I want to really consider You and Your greatness. When I do, I can praise You for who You are. Compared to You, I should feel humbled. I want to be gentle and kind instead of proud and selfish. You're against the proud, and I don't want You to be against me! Please help me humbly remember who I am and who You are. In Jesus' name I pray, amen.

Becoming a Good Friend

A friend loves at all times.
A brother is born to share troubles.
PROVERBS 17:17

Lord, You've blessed me with friends who fill my life with happiness and laughter. I'm so thankful for these friendships! I pray that I'll be a good friend to my friends. I want to become the kind of friend I'd like to have. Please help me be loving and thoughtful. Even when it might seem uncomfortable, I want to share my friends' troubles by being caring and a good listener. If my friends need help that's beyond something I can offer, could You please guide me in the right direction? Please fill me with Your wisdom and help me be a good, good friend. In Jesus' name I pray, amen.

Strength in Weakness

*He answered me, "I am all you need.
I give you My loving-favor. My power
works best in weak people." I am
happy to be weak and have troubles
so I can have Christ's power in me.*

2 CORINTHIANS 12:9

Father, it's a huge relief to know that Your power is perfected in weakness, because I'm feeling pretty weak! I know I can't do everything on my own. I don't have enough ideas or inspiration. I'm not that good at everything. I doubt I have enough strength or energy or courage. I want You to use me in any way, but I admit I feel like I don't have so much to offer. Use my weaknesses in any way, and help me do amazing things through You and Your power. I'm so grateful You never expect me to be perfect. Instead, You let me be myself, and then You perform great works. Thank You!

WHere'S your Trust?

*I lift up my soul to You, O Lord. O my God,
I trust in You. Do not let me be ashamed.
Do not let those who fight against me win.*
PSALM 25:1–2

Lord, I don't always trust You completely. Sometimes I doubt that Your way for me is the best way. Other times I try to take matters into my own hands and trust myself. That's just foolishness though! Who am I to trust in myself, when I know all my failures and flaws? When I put my trust in You, everything changes. You're all-powerful. You're all-knowing. You're worthy of my praise. I can put my trust in You, knowing You won't let me be put to shame. You'll protect me, and You'll lead the way. As I follow You, You'll guide me into good places. I can take comfort and rest in You, and for that, I'm grateful. Thank You! I love You!

FiLLED WiTH GOOD THiNGS

Our hope comes from God. May He fill you with joy and peace because of your trust in Him. May your hope grow stronger by the power of the Holy Spirit.

ROMANS 15:13

Father, You have a wonderful way of heaping so much goodness into my life. If I stop and think about all the good things You do for me, whether they're big or little, I'm thankful! You're the God of hope. I can believe in You and expect You to work in my life. I can trust You'll fill me with *all* joy and *all* peace—not just a little. When You bless me with joy and peace, I'll be filled to overflowing with hope in You. Please help me share Your joy and peace and hope with people around me. In Jesus' name I pray, amen.

Being Near God

But as for me, it is good to be near God.
I have made the Lord God my safe place.
So I may tell of all the things You have done.

PSALM 73:28

Lord God, You're a safe place in a dangerous world. I can trust in You completely and You'll keep me safe and secure. When I choose to come near to You, You'll come near to me. Since it's such a good thing to be near You, I want to get closer and closer. As I get nearer to You and get to know You better, I'll be able to clearly see so many of the things You've done in my life and in the world around me. I want to tell other people all that You do for me! Amen.

HeLPeD!

"For I am the Lord your God Who holds your right hand, and Who says to you, 'Do not be afraid. I will help you.'"
ISAIAH 41:13

Father, it's such a huge comfort to know You hold my hand and never leave me. You help me. Because of You, I don't have to fear. And I don't have to feel lonely, since You're always there for me. Thank You! I want to trust You and Your loving, caring protection for me. Sometimes I feel pretty helpless and afraid, so knowing that You're there for me is a huge relief. I need Your help! Please help me relax as I trust You more and more. I'm so thankful I don't have to live a life full of worry or fear, because You're in control. In Jesus' name I pray, amen.

Not Caving In

But even if you suffer for doing what is right, you will be happy. Do not be afraid or troubled by what they may do to make it hard for you.
1 PETER 3:14

God, You are perfect in Your goodness and kindness. I want to be so much like You, even if it feels tough or almost impossible. No matter what the world might say, please help me stand strong and not cave in to pressure. When something is right, I want to do it. And if something is wrong, I want to stand for my beliefs and not give in. I don't want to live in fear of what others think or do to me. I want to focus on You and live a life that's holy and pleasing to You and You alone. Please give me the strength to do that, Lord. Amen.

Trusting the God of Miracles

The Lord gave them peace on every side,
just as He had promised their fathers. Not
one of all those who hated them could
stand in front of them. The Lord gave all
those who hated them into their hand.

JOSHUA 21:44

Lord, You're so good! You always keep Your promises, and You always protect Your people. I'm thankful for examples of Your faithfulness in the Bible. You're the same God today as You were then. Even when I feel like I'm in the middle of a fight or my enemies are super scary, I can trust You to work all things out for good. I love You, and I trust You. I can hardly wait to see the ways You'll work in my life. I want to trust You more and more every day. You're the God of miracles, and I worship You. Amen.

You Do You

Jesus said, "If I want this one to wait until I come, what is that to you? You follow Me."
JOHN 21:22

Father, You know how much I compare myself with other people. What I really wish I could do is focus on Your plan for my life. You've gifted me in a unique way. No one else is like me! You have very unique plans and purposes for my life. I know You're doing lots of other things in everyone else's lives—that's what You do! But what is it to me if You choose different stories and twists and turns for every single person? Help me focus on You alone and to follow You with my whole heart. Thank You for my life's one-of-a-kind adventure! In Jesus' name I pray, amen.

He Loves Me Anyway

The Lord has looked down from heaven on the sons of men, to see if there are any who understand and look for God.

PSALM 14:2

Lord, You see and know absolutely everything. You search human hearts and know what's truly inside, including every person's thoughts. When it comes to You, I don't have to try to pretend I'm someone I'm not, because You know me completely. I'm sorry for the ways I mess up over and over again. Lord, I want to focus more on You and less on myself. I know this won't happen overnight. In fact, it's something I'll deal with my entire life. But You know everything good and bad about me, and You love me anyway. I love You and want to be devoted to You. I want to look for You every day. I love You!

Treasured

He said, "O man who is loved very much,
do not be afraid. May peace be with you.
Be strong and have strength of heart."
And when he had spoken to me, I received
strength, and said, "May my lord speak,
for you have given me strength."
DANIEL 10:19

Oh Lord, to know that You treasure Your loved
ones means so much to me. It's a comfort to
know I don't have to be afraid. I don't have to
live in fear, because You're the all-powerful God.
You give courage, and You walk with those You
love. When I feel afraid, I want to find courage
in You alone. I don't want to live in fear anymore.
I'm so thankful that in You I can be strong and
courageous. I want to step out in faith, knowing
that You will guide and protect me. You will give
me peace. Thank You!

Follow His Way

"Follow My teachings and learn from Me. I am gentle and do not have pride. You will have rest for your souls."

MATTHEW 11:29

Jesus, You offer me forever life with You if and when I believe in You. But instead of only giving something for eternity, You also offer a great gift of rest right now. It's not just a rest like I'm feeling relaxed right now, but a deep soul rest filled with peace. The way You gently offer it is so caring, but this kind of invitation also means I need to respond. I can choose to take Your rest. I can choose to learn from You and follow Your teachings. Or I can choose to ignore Your offer or push it to the side until I feel like I'm prepared. I want to drop everything that stands in the way, Lord, and follow You. Amen.

THiNKiNg BeFore DoiNg

Watch the path of your feet,
and all your ways will be sure.
PROVERBS 4:26

Father, when You created humans, You never intended us to just react to whatever happens in our lives. When I pay attention to the way I'm going, I'll have a better life. It can be hard to think through the things I do every day though. I'm tempted to take the easy way and do whatever feels natural or what others pressure me to do. When this happens, please remind me that I have a choice in what I do and the way I respond to everything. Please help me know what's right and wrong. Please help me think through the good and bad outcomes of my choices. I want to watch the path of my feet so my ways will be sure. In Jesus' name I pray, amen.

WHO'S THE BOSS?

If your sinful old self is the boss over your mind, it leads to death. But if the Holy Spirit is the boss over your mind, it leads to life and peace.

ROMANS 8:6

Lord, You've been so good to offer me life and peace instead of doubt and misery. If I want to choose peace—and I do!—I need to be willing to let the Holy Spirit lead me. He needs to become my boss. I need to not only listen to Him, but also obey Him. If I choose to sin over and over again because it seems fun or feels good, I'll become numb to what I'm doing wrong and deaf to the quiet way the Spirit speaks to me. I don't want to drown out His voice with a bunch of sin! Please help me make the hard choices to follow You and Your right, life-giving way. Amen.

Frustrated With Frustration

My soul is in great suffering.
But You, O Lord, how long?
PSALM 6:3

Oh Lord, when I go through hard times, it feels like my troubles will go on forever. I don't feel right, and I can't stop thinking about my struggles. I'm not being overdramatic when I tell You that I feel like I'm suffering. Could You please help me? Could You please bring an end to all my discouragement? I wish everything could be better right now. Sometimes, though, I just need to learn to wait for You through all the ugliness. I need to learn to trust You and be patient. I can keep hoping that You'll make all things right. Please help me patiently keep going even when I feel miserable. Please help me experience Your love in new and real ways every day. In Your name I pray, amen.

Paying Attention

*"If only you had listened to My Laws! Then
your peace would have been like a river
and your right-standing with God would
have been like the waves of the sea."*

ISAIAH 48:18

Lord, You're so kind to offer me peace, especially
when Your peace goes on and on like a river! And
You promise me right standing with You that will
keep coming and coming, as constant and sure
as the waves of the sea. Thank You! I need to do
something so I can experience Your peace and
being right in Your eyes. I need to pay attention
to Your commands and actually know them. I
may not always think about reading the Bible,
but when I do read it, please help me really think
about what is written and let it change my life.
In Jesus' name I pray, amen.

Questions and Answers

Jesus said to them, "Why are you afraid?
Why do you have doubts in your hearts?"
LUKE 24:38

Jesus, when You lived on this earth, You knew exactly what was in people's hearts. You understood what they wrestled with, thought, and felt. The great thing is, You helped people deal with their thoughts and feelings. You didn't preach bossy messages that made people feel bad about themselves, but You asked questions. When Your disciples were afraid, You didn't scold them for their fear, but You asked why they were afraid. You knew that fear is tied to doubt, but You didn't criticize their doubts. You simply asked why they had doubts in their hearts. If You were here today, Lord, You could ask me the same questions. Why am I afraid? Why do I have doubts in my heart? I want to think these questions over and give my fear and doubt to You. Amen.

Peace and Rest

"See, a son will be born to you, who will be a man of peace. I will give him peace from all those who hate him on every side. His name will be Solomon. And I will give peace and quiet to Israel in his days."

1 CHRONICLES 22:9

Lord, just as You give peace and rest as a great gift, You also allow conflict and disagreements to happen. Please guard me from trouble. Please help me become a peacemaker. Help me listen to both sides of a story and help others calm down. Instead of picking a fight or always looking for a reason to disagree or complain, I'd love to find the good in a person or situation. Please help me smooth rough situations with my family and friends. Could You please help me? I love You, I trust You, and I want to be Your peacemaker in this stress-filled world. Amen.

Harvesting What You Plant

*Those who plant seeds of peace will
gather what is right and good.*
JAMES 3:18

Father, trying to make peace in this world really isn't that easy. In fact, sometimes peace seems almost impossible—especially when others disagree with me. While You never said that keeping peace was easy, Your Word does teach that a lot of good comes out of it. If I plant seeds of peace, I'll gather a right and good harvest. My attitude and words plant seeds. Since everything I do is like as a seed, why not just plant goodness? If I plant a crop of nastiness, cruelty, anger, disgust, or hatred, I'll harvest something pretty awful. But when I plant peace, kindness, gentleness, joy, patience, or love, my harvest will be right and good. Please help me see the peaceful way and choose to live it! Amen.

Living With Liars

They do not speak peace. But they make up lies against those who are quiet in the land.
PSALM 35:20

Father, I hate it when people lie about me. I just wish everyone would treat me fairly and kindly! But that's just not the way this world works. Even if people are mean to me for no reason at all, please help me respond in a way that honors You. I really don't like experiencing conflict. Please teach me something from this! Even if I learn how I don't want to be treated or how I don't want to treat others, those are good lessons that can change my life. Please keep me from sharing rumors or saying outright lies about other people. I don't want to wrongly accuse, and I don't want to fall into the trap of speaking poorly about others. Please help me!

NeeD Some ADvice?

*Oil and perfume make the heart glad,
so are a man's words sweet to his friend.*

PROVERBS 27:9

Lord, sometimes when my friends ask me for advice, I don't know what to say. I don't want to lead them in the wrong direction, because I want the best for my friends! Please help me remember that my advice doesn't have to be perfectly wise. In fact, I can really help out just by listening to my friend talk. I want to show that I care, even if I'm not exactly sure what kind of advice would be good. Please give me wisdom! Help me see my friend's situation clearly and know what to say. Please help me to look at things through Your eyes and be able to give good advice. In Your name I pray, amen.

COME AWAY AND REST

He said to them, "Come away from the people. Be by yourselves and rest." There were many people coming and going. They had had no time even to eat.

MARK 6:31

Jesus, when You walked on this earth, You knew how important it was to get away from crowds. You got away to pray, and when You and Your disciples were in the middle of a really busy time, You invited them to come away and rest a little while. It's so nice to realize that You cared about them so much and knew they needed to rest, recharge, and take time to eat! The same can be true for me. When I'm constantly surrounded by people and things to do, I get worn out. I need time to get away by myself and rest. I need to take some time out to enjoy a meal. Always running from activity to activity isn't healthy for my body or my soul. Like Your disciples, I want to rest with You. Amen.

Safely Set on High

"He makes my feet like the feet of a deer. He sets me safe on high places."
2 SAMUEL 22:34

Lord, thank You for the many ways You care for me and protect me even when I don't even realize it. You set me safely on high places that are out of reach from danger. And You make my feet like the feet of a deer—quick and nimble and amazingly able to leap out of harm's way at a moment's notice. If I only relied on myself and my own judgment and ability to stay safe, I think I'd be more like a sloth—slow and a little unaware of what's really going on. But You're my great protector. You do so many loving, kind, and helpful things for me that I don't even see or realize. But You care for me in amazing ways. Thank You! I love You!

GOD'S GOOD GIFT OF PEACE

*The peace of God is much greater
than the human mind can understand.
This peace will keep your hearts
and minds through Christ Jesus.*

PHILIPPIANS 4:7

Lord God, You give an amazing gift of peace. I can't understand the way it makes me feel, but I know it calms me down. You fill my heart with Your peace so I feel hopeful and relaxed as I trust You. And when I let You fill my mind with Your peace, my worries disappear. It's pretty amazing, actually. Experiencing Your peace is a great way for me to tell if I'm truly trusting in You or trying to solve all my own problems. When I feel really stressed out and don't experience Your peace, it's a giveaway that I'm focused on the things of this world. Please help me give all my cares and worries to You! Amen.

So Much Good

O Lord my God, many are the great works You have done, and Your thoughts toward us. No one can compare with You! If I were to speak and tell of them, there would be too many to number.

PSALM 40:5

Lord, You are so very good to me! It amazes me to think of all the wonderful things You've done in my life. You've given me so many great gifts. Without needing to brag to anyone else, You've given me some pretty great talents! When I think about the people in my life who love and care for me, I'm thankful for the way You use them to make me a better person. When I consider the different moments in my life when You've done really good things for me, I'm grateful! Thank You!

GIVING NEW STRENGTH

For the high and honored One Who lives forever, Whose name is Holy, says, "I live in the high and holy place. And I also live with those who are sorry for their sins and have turned from them and are not proud. I give new strength to the spirit of those without pride, and also to those whose hearts are sorry for their sins."

ISAIAH 57:15

Father, You're holy. You're set apart from everyone and everything, yet You sent Your Son into this world as a human. Plus Your Holy Spirit lives in all people who put their trust in You. I love the way You've chosen me to be Yours. So much in this world seems to try to get me down. I get worn out and feel tempted to worry. But You're ready to give me new strength. You give life—as the Creator, You give physical life; and through Jesus, You give spiritual life. Thank You!

Trust vs. Trouble

"Do not let your heart be troubled.
You have put your trust in God,
put your trust in Me also."

JOHN 14:1

Lord Jesus, I'm so thankful You're trustworthy. You've proved Yourself to be faithful, and I can put my trust in You. When I do, I don't have to be worried or afraid! My heart doesn't have to be troubled. I can rest from all my concerns and feel at peace. I don't have to feel like I'm the one needing to do all the work or make sure things work out the right way. I can trust that You're working out all the details in a wonderful way. Even when life's uncertain, You've got it all under control. I don't have to worry! That is a huge gift that makes me happy. Thank You!

THE UGLINESS OF FIGHTING

A dry piece of food with peace and quiet is better than a house full of food with fighting.
PROVERBS 17:1

Father, I'll never get along with everyone, and not everyone will get along with me. Just because I should expect conflict, though, it doesn't make living through it any easier. In fact, fighting feels pretty awful. The proverb is right: it's better to eat just a dry piece of food in a peaceful, quiet place, instead of feasting on all sorts of delicious food in a home where people are fighting. Could You please help me remember this the next time I am tempted to start or continue an argument with my family members? I don't want to start a fight, and I don't want to become the sort of person who needs to get the last word. Help me make peace in my home a priority. In Jesus' name I pray, amen.

CHOOSING GOOD

Turn away from what is sinful. Do what is good. Look for peace and go after it.
1 PETER 3:11

Lord, every day I make choices between what is right and wrong. All the time I need to choose things like what to eat, what to say, what to watch, what to talk about, what to listen to, how well I do my chores or my schoolwork, and how I treat other people. Please help me realize these tiny matters mean something. I could choose sin, or I could turn away from what I know is wrong. I want to do good! Even when it feels tough, and even if a lot of people are upset or disappointed with my decision, please help me do what's good. I want to do what's right in Your eyes. In Your name I pray, amen.

Saved, Not Shaken

My soul is quiet and waits for God alone.
He is the One Who saves me. He alone is
my rock and the One Who saves me. He
is my strong place. I will not be shaken.
PSALM 62:1–2

Oh Lord, so often I try to do things all by myself. I'm impatient. I want to rush through life. I want to be busy and do, do, do all the time. It's hard to wait. But You're the One who saves me. You're the One I can and should wait for and trust. You're my rock. You're my strong place. Because of You, I don't need to worry or fear. I can stand strong in You. If I depended only on myself, I'd be worried and shaken and upset. But I can depend on You. I can put all my confidence in You, because You'll never, ever let me down. Thank You!

SHout for Joy!

Sing for joy, O heavens! Be glad, O earth!
Break out into songs of joy, O mountains!
For the Lord has comforted His people. He
will have loving-pity on His suffering people.
ISAIAH 49:13

Lord, You're so very good! All creation can re-
joice in You! You comfort Your people. When the
people You love suffer, You shower them with
Your love. You look on me with kindness and love.
But I don't stop to marvel at Your great love and
patience and faithfulness. I forget how good
Your goodness is or how kind Your kindness is.
I need to praise You! I can shout and sing for
joy over the wonderful ways You work in my life.
I want to rejoice in You! I worship You, Mighty
God! I praise Your name, my Lord and Savior!

Not My Own Power

What I had to say when I preached was not in big sounding words of man's wisdom. But it was given in the power of the Holy Spirit. In this way, you do not have faith in Christ because of the wisdom of men. You have faith in Christ because of the power of God.

1 CORINTHIANS 2:4–5

Father, I know I'm not the best at everything. Even if I try my hardest, I might fail. And sometimes, I feel pretty weak and powerless. I want You to use me in this world though. Even with all my failures and flaws, would You please strengthen me? Could You please give me the words and energy to do Your work? I know I can only do so much—or, actually, so little—on my own. But through Your power, I can hardly wait to see all that You will do through me! Amen.

Comfort after Troubles

You have shown me many troubles of all kinds. But You will make me strong again. And You will bring me up again from deep in the earth. Add to my greatness, and turn to comfort me.

PSALM 71:20–21

Father, You've never promised a problem-free life. When I'm going through a really rough time and it feels like the challenges and bad news just won't stop, those struggles won't last forever. You'll restore my life. You'll increase my honor. What might be sweetest of all is the way You'll comfort me. I won't have to feel like I'm all on my own dealing with my problems, but You'll comfort me with Your love. After going through hard times, the good times will seem even better. For that, I'm thankful! Thanks for never leaving me and for carrying me through all of my life—in good times *and* bad times. Amen.

Making Every Effort

Be at peace with all men. Live a holy life. No one will see the Lord without having that kind of life.

HEBREWS 12:14

Lord, because You're perfect in goodness, it makes sense that Your followers should try to be like You. There's one big thing though. I'm imperfect. You already know that, but I get frustrated by my failures. Even though I don't always make the right choices, I still should keep trying. I don't have to give up just because I mess up. Instead, please help me try again. Please help me really try to live in a way that shows my love and honor for You. Please help me live in peace with others, especially people who think and behave so much differently than I do. Instead of focusing on our differences, I want to love them like You do. Amen.

Strong and Courageous

Be strong. Be strong in heart,
all you who hope in the Lord.
PSALM 31:24

Father, sometimes I feel really nervous and uncertain and afraid. I don't know what will happen. And sometimes I really dread what I know I need to do. In those times when I feel like my courage has vanished, please strengthen me in an amazing way. When I feel scared, please give me courage to do what's right and good. I want to trust You. I want my heart and soul and mind to take courage in You. I don't need to trust in myself or my own understanding of things. Instead, I choose to trust in You. You are my tower of strength. You're the Rock that won't be moved. I worship You alone! Amen.

Quiet Trust

The Lord God, the Holy One of Israel,
has said, "In turning away from sin and in
rest, you will be saved. Your strength will
come by being quiet and by trusting."
ISAIAH 30:15

Lord God, You've taught that when I rest in You and turn away from sin, I'll be saved. Strength will come by being quiet and trusting. I have a choice either to listen to You or to turn to my own way. If I don't trust You, if I keep my sinful habits, and if I work, work, work to try to save myself, I won't be saved at all. I want to trust You! I want to be still and know that You are God. I want to trust You completely. I want to turn away from what I think is my own wisdom or the world's wisdom and turn to You. Help me quiet my soul and wait for You. Amen.

WHY Worry?

*"Which of you can make himself
a little taller by worrying?"*
MATTHEW 6:27

Jesus, You know that worry doesn't change a thing. I can't solve problems by worrying. In fact, if anything, worrying just piles on stress. I want to be worry-free! Deep down I think it would be great to have such a strong and certain faith in You, so I wouldn't fear anything that comes my way. Please help me trust You more and more. I want to keep my eyes on You and not what's happening around me. Please help me see the way You work wonders all the time, even when it may not feel like it. Thank You for loving me like You do and freeing me from worry. In Your name I pray, amen.

Quiet DOWN!

*The words of the wise heard in
quiet are better than the loud
words of a ruler among fools.*
ECCLESIASTES 9:17

Father, sometimes it's easy for me to lose
my temper. I don't think before I say things.
Sometimes I get so upset I scream and shout
and throw a fit. Could You please help me
grow out of these temper tantrums? Could
You please help me get my emotions under
control? I don't want to get upset, and I don't
want to hurt others' feelings by what I say or
do when I'm angry. Please help me grow in
self-control. Please calm me down. I'd love to
grow up in wisdom and outgrow my foolishness. Please help my words and emotions and
reactions reflect my love and respect for You
and the way You're working in my heart. In
Jesus' name I pray, amen.

Let Your Light Shine

"You are the light of the world. You cannot hide a city that is on a mountain. Men do not light a lamp and put it under a basket. They put it on a table so it gives light to all in the house. Let your light shine in front of men. Then they will see the good things you do and will honor your Father Who is in heaven."
MATTHEW 5:14–16

Father, I know You're the one true God. I know that, through Jesus, You've provided a rescue from the consequences of sin. I know Your Holy Spirit lives in me. All of that wonderful truth lights me up. I don't want to keep Your light hidden from others. I want other people to honor You because of the good things I do. I want to shine like a light in this world. I love You, Lord!

MY RELiaNCe

O my Strength, I will sing praises to You.
For God is my strong place and the God
Who shows me loving-kindness.

PSALM 59:17

God, You are my God! I can and do rely on You.
You're my safe, strong place. No matter what
happens in the world around me, I can cling
to You. My strength is found in You. I'm so glad
You're faithful. Everything in this world may be
uncertain, but You are certain. Everything in
this world may change, but You're unchanging.
Without You, I'd feel like my whole life was shaky,
but because of You I don't have to fear. Lord,
I know I can rely completely on You. When I'm
tempted to rely on myself, please help me step
back and remember who You are. I can rely on
You, my strong place. In Your name I pray, amen.

It's Gardening Time!

"Plant what is right and good for yourselves. Gather the fruit of lasting love. Break up your ground that has not been plowed. For it is time to look for the Lord, until He comes and pours His saving power on you."

HOSEA 10:12

Father, good, right living doesn't need to be a mystery. In fact, You explain it in the Bible so I can understand. I want to plant good habits and decisions in my life that will result in what is right. If there's any part of my life that's hardened by sin, please help me break it up. I want the soil of my heart to be good so when You rain Your righteousness on me, all that I've planted will bloom and grow. I want my obedience and love for You to affect every single part of my life. Amen.

COME

*Jesus was walking by the Sea of Galilee.
He saw Simon and his brother Andrew
putting a net into the sea. They were
fishermen. Jesus said to them, "Follow
Me. I will make you fish for men!" At once
they left their nets and followed Him.*

MARK 1:16–18

Jesus, when You walked on this earth, people knew You were different from all others. There was something so remarkable about You. You were God—in the flesh! All You needed to do was say the word "Come!" and people left everything they knew to follow You. Today You ask me to come and follow You too. I want to leave everything—including my belongings—to follow You. As I follow You, please teach me how to be a fisher of people. How can I bring others into a relationship with You? Please help! Amen.

Strength of Heart

*Say to those whose heart is afraid,
"Have strength of heart, and do not be
afraid. See, your God will come ready
to punish. He will come to make sinners
pay for their sins, but He will save you."*

ISAIAH 35:4

Father, I worship You as the One true God who
created all things and knows all things. You
hold all things together. You know who ac-
cepts and trusts You and who doesn't. You've
promised to save those who believe in You.
Even when I feel afraid of what's happening
around me, I can have a strong heart. Fear
seems to be such a normal part of this life, but
I don't have to fear! I can and do trust that
You'll save me, just like You've promised. Please
help me do what's right in Your sight. I want to
find my courage in You. Amen.

WHAT IS RIGHT

*Turn away from the sinful things young
people want to do. Go after what is
right. Have a desire for faith and love
and peace. Do this with those who
pray to God from a clean heart.*

2 TIMOTHY 2:22

Lord, there's so much temptation to do things
that won't please You. It's no surprise to You
that there are so many ways I could choose to
sin. But I want to go after what's right, even if it
doesn't always seem fun or popular. Even when
young people choose sin, please help me turn
away from that. I want to have a clean heart
in Your sight. You can help me grow in love
and peace. Would You please do it? Could You
please help my faith grow? I want to be more
like You, but it's hard in this world. Amen.

No Stumbling

Those who love Your Law have great peace, and nothing will cause them to be hurt in their spirit.

PSALM 119:165

Father, Your Word is absolutely true. It's not like You created people and then left us on our own to try to figure everything out. Through the Bible, You've told us specifically what to do and what not to do. If and when we follow You and obey, our lives are filled with blessings and joy. I don't want to worry. I don't want to get all stressed out. I want to live every day with a peace of mind that You're in control. Because of You and Your goodness, I don't have to fear. Because of You and the way Your Word lays out the right ways of living, I don't need to fumble and stumble around. Thank You!

Peaceful Rest

*Then my people will live in a place of peace,
in safe homes, and in quiet resting places.*
ISAIAH 32:18

Lord, I don't have to worry about what might happen to me. You'll give me rest! No matter what people say or do to me, You'll still give me peace. You protect me like nothing or no one else. I don't have to fear. I also don't have to stick to myself, soak up all Your peace and rest, and do nothing. No, I can boldly go out into the world for You. I can be the hands and feet of Jesus every day to the people around me. I can treat others with Your kindness and gentleness. I can love the unlovable because of You. I can be so full of Your joy and peace that it spills out of my life to those around me. Amen.

Happy!

*I am not saying I need anything. I have
learned to be happy with whatever I have.*
PHILIPPIANS 4:11

Father, You're the giver of all good gifts. Thank
You for all You've given me! Sometimes I take
Your good gifts for granted. I might even think
I want different things. But when I keep in mind
that You have a special, one-of-a-kind purpose
for my life, I remember You've created me in
a unique way. I want to be happy with whatever You've given me. Please help me see the
difference between wanting something versus
needing something. And please help me see
how very much I already have. I want to be
willing to share Your blessings and gifts with
others. In Your name I pray, amen.

New Life

"The Lord your God is with you, a Powerful One Who wins the battle. He will have much joy over you. With His love He will give you new life. He will have joy over you with loud singing."

ZEPHANIAH 3:17

Lord God, sometimes I feel so weak and helpless, like my life doesn't matter in the big scheme of things. What can a holy God like You really accomplish through *my* life? Do I help or hurt Your work in this world? No matter what I feel, the Bible tells the truth about how You find joy in me. Joy! So much joy, in fact, that You have joy over me with loud singing. With Your love for me, You give me new life. Your joy and love are wonderful things! I'm so thankful I can trust in You and get the new life You're willing to give me. I love You, Lord!

Keep Looking to Jesus

All these many people who have had faith in God are around us like a cloud. Let us put every thing out of our lives that keeps us from doing what we should. Let us keep running in the race that God has planned for us. Let us keep looking to Jesus. Our faith comes from Him and He is the One Who makes it perfect.

HEBREWS 12:1–2

Jesus, I want to keep looking to You! It's so tricky in this world though. I'm pulled in different directions. I face temptations. I get tangled up in sins until I trip and fall. I want to break free from life's distractions and focus on You. If my life is a marathon, help me keep going when I get tired. Help me not to get distracted by what's happening in other people's lives or in the world around me. I want to stay focused on You!

EVEN WHEN you SLeep

*You rise up early, and go to bed late,
and work hard for your food, all for
nothing. For the Lord gives to His
loved ones even while they sleep.*

PSALM 127:2

Lord, it's so comforting to know that I don't have to work for my blessings! You give to me so generously, and I don't need to do a thing to earn or deserve Your goodness. When I'm tempted to get up early and stay up late just to cram in everything I need to do, please remind me that all of that effort is meaningless. You love me, and You give to me, even when I sleep. That might be one of the sweetest things I've realized in a long time: You choose to give me good gifts even while I sleep! I don't have to do a thing. Thank You!

Wise or Foolish

*Understanding is a well of life
to him who has it, but to speak
strong words to fools is of no use.*

PROVERBS 16:22

Father, some days I just want to have fun. I want to forget about consequences and totally enjoy myself and make unplanned choices. Life seems so much more fun that way! But the thing is, the more foolish choices I make, the more of a fool I'll become. I'll also need to face up to a bunch of consequences that could be avoided. Even if it makes me less than popular with my friends, please help me use my brain before doing things. Help me grow in wisdom so I can make wise, responsible choices. As I do that, please help me have fun too. Following the rules or making the best choices doesn't need to mean that life is totally boring. Please help me trust You for what's right. Amen.

Do You Have Life?

*This is the word He spoke: God gave us life
that lasts forever, and this life is in His Son.
He that has the Son has life. He that does
not have the Son of God does not have life.*

1 JOHN 5:11–12

Father, thank You for explaining how I can have
forever life with You. If I have the Son of God, I
have eternal life. If I don't have the Son of God,
I don't have eternal life. It's that simple. Just
in case I'm unsure if I do have Him, right now
I'll say: I absolutely believe that Jesus is Lord. I
believe You raised Him from the dead and He's
alive today. I believe I can spend forever with
You only through Jesus. It's not the good things
I do, and it doesn't matter if I try really hard. It
doesn't come by any other name or religion. It's
only through Your Son. Amen.

Searching for Wisdom

Happy is the man who finds wisdom, and the man who gets understanding. For it is better than getting silver and fine gold. She is worth more than stones of great worth. Nothing you can wish for compares with her.

PROVERBS 3:13–15

Father, over and over Your Word tells about how priceless wisdom is. It's better to be wise than a fool; and making wise choices will bring wonderful results in my life. Even if wisdom is great, when I see people around me living for the moment and doing what feels good, it's tempting to follow the crowd. If something is foolish, please help me notice right away and find wisdom's hidden treasure. While it's hard to see that right now as I try to figure out good choices for my life, please help me begin to see how I'll change for the better because of wisdom. Amen.

The Gift of Peace

*May the Lord of peace give you His peace
at all times. The Lord be with you all.*
2 THESSALONIANS 3:16

Lord, peace seems like such a nice thought. With peace, I don't have to worry if anyone's upset with me; I'm not in the middle of disagreements; and I don't even need to feel stressed out about my future. Everything just seems nice and calm. I feel refreshed from the inside out. This kind of peace doesn't need to only be a dream though. You're the Lord of peace, and You can give peace. The peace You offer isn't a short-lived, one-time offer. You give peace at all times and in every way. Thanks for Your peace! I don't understand it, but I love the way it makes me feel. In Your name I pray, amen.

BeHaViNG MySeLf

*Look at the man without blame. And watch
the man who is right and good. For the man
of peace will have much family to follow him.*
PSALM 37:37

Father, I don't always like other people telling
me to behave myself. Sometimes—okay, *most
times!*—I like doing what I feel like doing. But
if I make right choices, I'm on a good path in
life. When I seek peace with other people and
in this world, I can look forward to my future.
Could You please help me with this kind of right,
good, peaceful living? Because it's hard! I don't
always feel like living that way, and it's hard to
not argue and disagree with people, especially when they're treating me badly. It's hard to
behave myself so I can live a life without blame.
But with You and Your help, I can do anything.
Please help me!

He's the One

O Lord, You will give us peace,
for You have done all our works for us.
ISAIAH 26:12

Lord, You're the One who gives peace. And You're the One who has plans and purposes for my life and makes them happen. When I really believe this, it frees me up so much! I don't have to be consumed with trying to do more and be more. I don't need to obsess over doing my best at school or what I can do to help my friendships. Ultimately I need to trust You. When I start feeling worried and stressed, I need to stop and pray. You're the Difference Maker. I can take a deep breath and trust You. I know You'll lead me along paths of peace to accomplish what You have planned. Please help me follow You! Amen.

DON'T BE SO JUDGY!

Only God can say what is right or wrong. He made the Law. He can save or put to death. How can we say if our brother is right or wrong?

JAMES 4:12

Father, it's so easy for me to judge other people. All it takes is looking at other people, and instantly I start comparing them. I notice so much so quickly, from clothing choices to hairstyles. I notice attitudes and the way other people talk or walk. It's like I can't turn off my brain. And instead of just noticing things, I let it all shape my opinion. So often, those opinions turn into judgment. But I don't know what's going on in a person's life or heart or mind until I stop to get to know her and actually ask questions. Do I usually do that? Not as often as I should. Please help me stop judging other people and be more understanding. Amen.

THe Giver of Rest

But now the Lord my God has given me rest on every side. There is no trouble or anything bad happening.

1 KINGS 5:4

Lord my God, You're the giver of good gifts! And You're the giver of rest and peace. Just like You gave King Solomon rest and peace during his reign, could You please give me rest? Could You please fill my life and relationships with peace? I'd love a break from trouble, and I would love for nothing bad to happen. I know every life includes some kind of trouble and challenge, because that's what shapes a person. And I know You can bring goodness and growth out of any conflict and crisis. But I'd still prefer Your rest. Please help me trust You more every day. In Jesus' name I pray, amen.

WHEN I DON'T WANT TO LOVE

"You have heard that it has been said, 'You must love your neighbor and hate those who hate you.' But I tell you, love those who hate you. . . . Pray for those who do bad things to you and who make it hard for you."

MATTHEW 5:43–44

Father, when I know someone doesn't like me or says awful things about me, I get pretty mad and defensive. *Who do they think they are? Why don't they see things my way?* My natural reaction is to react in anger and hurt. But that's not what Jesus taught. Jesus taught something so uncomfortable: loving people who hate you. He specifically said to love my enemies and pray for people who do bad things to me. This is really hard to hear and even harder to do. I want to obey You though. Please help me love others, whether I'm loving my neighbors or my enemies. Amen.

Comfort in Suffering

Your Word has given me new life.
This is my comfort in my suffering.
PSALM 119:50

O Lord, some days are just bad. I know I probably should try to find good in everything, but sometimes I feel pretty down. A lot of things can make me feel so depressed, and it's hard to find a bright spot. You can be my bright spot though. You can be my good thing. When I'm suffering, I can find comfort in Your promises. In Your Word, You promise You'll never leave me. You have called me by name. I am Yours! Those promises save my life like nothing else. Please help me find comfort in them even right now. In Your name I pray, amen.

WHat's your Treasure?

"Do not gather together for yourself riches of this earth. They will be eaten by bugs and become rusted. Men can break in and steal them. Gather together riches in heaven where they will not be eaten by bugs or become rusted. Men cannot break in and steal them. For wherever your riches are, your heart will be there also."
MATTHEW 6:19–21

Father, it's really easy to focus on the things of this world. I see so much every day, and I'm tempted to buy so many things. It's like all I see around me are bigger and better things. I'm so used to seeing advertisements and being encouraged to want more. So much of this world focuses on storing up belongings here on earth. But You've asked me to store up treasure that won't fall apart. Instead, if I store up treasures in heaven, they'll last forever. Father, please help me treasure forever things instead of earthly things. Amen.

Safety in the Storm

God is our safe place and our strength.
He is always our help when we are in
trouble. So we will not be afraid, even if
the earth is shaken and the mountains
fall into the center of the sea, and even
if its waters go wild with storm and the
mountains shake with its action.

PSALM 46:1–3

Lord, I get scared when I hear about natural disasters. Earthquakes and hurricanes are scary things, and when I hear about disasters happening around the world, I wonder what I would do if I was in the middle of an epic storm. The amazing thing about You, though, is that You're my safe place. You're my strength. When I'm in trouble, You're always my help. So when scary things happen, I don't have to worry about any of it. You'll keep me safe. I choose to trust in You. Amen.

Safe

"And He will come and feed His flock in the strength of the Lord, in the great power of the name of the Lord His God. His people will live there and be safe, because at that time He will be great to the ends of the earth."

MICAH 5:4

Lord, I love the way Your Word describes Jesus all the way from the Old Testament through the New Testament. And I love the way He brings hope and comfort to His flock. Thank You that Jesus feeds His flock of followers in Your strength and the great power of Your name. Nothing on earth compares with that! When I start thinking about the cares and worries of this world, please help me remember Your greatness. My problems might seem like big deals right now, but because of You, I don't need to be concerned. Amen.

Set Apart

May the God of peace set you apart for Himself. May every part of you be set apart for God. May your spirit and your soul and your body be kept complete. May you be without blame when our Lord Jesus Christ comes again.

1 THESSALONIANS 5:23

Father, so often I feel like the world is trying to press me into some sort of pattern. I'm asked to think or speak a certain way and do specific things. If I'm not like the world, people make fun of me, either behind my back or to my face. It's like any time I try to be myself and stand up for my beliefs, someone tries to change me. But I don't want to be more like the world, Lord. I want to be more like You. I want You to set me apart for Yourself. In Your goodness and protection, please keep my mind, soul, and body complete. Amen.

Wait!

Wait for the Lord. Be strong. Let your heart be strong. Yes, wait for the Lord.
PSALM 27:14

Lord, waiting is so hard! I don't feel very patient, and I really don't like waiting for anything. I'd like almost instant results and answers. But You tell me to wait. It's even like Psalms answers my question: *Do I really have to wait?* Yes! Wait for the Lord. And so I'll wait for You, because You tell me to and I don't have much of a choice. Please give me strength in my waiting and strength as I learn to be patient. Please help my heart be courageous too. Strong and courageous are what I need to be, even when it feels so difficult. I trust You, and I love You. In Your name I pray, amen.

WHat WiLL RiGHt LiviNG Do?

The work of being right and good will
give peace. From the right and good
work will come quiet trust forever.
ISAIAH 32:17

Father, over and over in Your Word, You tell me
that right living, or righteousness, is what I should
choose. It's hard to choose to not go my own
way and choose Your way instead. When I do
choose righteousness, good things will come!
It's like I'm a fruit tree that will produce good
fruit. Right living produces peace, and that's so
much better than worry, fear, or struggle. Peace
is what I'd love. Right living doesn't just help me
experience peace, but I'll also have confidence,
security, and trust forever. That sounds amazing!
Could You please help me see the difference
between what's right and wrong? Thank You!
In Jesus' name I pray, amen.

Happy With What I Have

Keep your lives free from the love of money.
Be happy with what you have. God has said,
"I will never leave you or let you be alone."
HEBREWS 13:5

Lord, so much of this world screams at me to want more. I hear that I deserve to get what I want when I want it or that I can have it all. But those lies are so different from Your truth. I don't need more. I don't need different things or "upgraded" anything. I will keep surviving if I don't get what catches my eye. If I have to wait to get something, it won't be the end of the world. And even if I had it all—whatever "all" is—I still might not be completely satisfied. Instead of buying into what the world tells me, please help me be happy with what I have. Amen.

WHO ARE YOU PLEASING?

*When the ways of a man are pleasing
to the Lord, He makes even those who
hate him to be at peace with him.*

PROVERBS 16:7

Lord, I don't want to be a people pleaser. It's hard, though, because people demand so much from me, and a big part of me feels like I need to perform or make others happy. If I end up as a disappointment, will they love me as much? Will I find approval in their eyes? The huge truth bomb, though, is that I need to be concerned about pleasing You. Not people! When I please You, You do a great thing: You make people be at peace with me. It doesn't matter if they're people who love or hate me. You pave the way for me to experience peace. Thank You!

Every Kind of People

After this I saw many people. No one could tell how many there were. They were from every nation and from every family and from every kind of people and from every language. They were standing before the throne and before the Lamb. They were wearing white clothes and they held branches in their hands. And they were crying out with a loud voice, "We are saved from the punishment of sin by our God Who sits on the throne and by the Lamb!"

REVELATION 7:9–10

Jesus, You're the Lamb of God who takes away the sin of the world. When I think about what heaven will be like, I'm excited to praise You forever with people from every nation and language. You've called so many people to be Your own from all over the world. Even though we'll look and sound different, we'll all have one thing in common: we will praise You! Amen.

My Rescuer

He took me away from the powerful one who fights against me, and from those who hated me. They were too strong for me.

PSALM 18:17

Father, the Bible tells a lot of details of King David's life. It wasn't easy! He had so many enemies who hated him so much they wanted to kill him. Yet You protected him. You kept him safe. No matter what they plotted against David, You ruined their plans so that he lived to be an old man. When hard times come in my life—and they will!—please remind me that You're my protector. You'll rescue me. You'll ruin the plans of my enemies. You'll even keep me safe from people who hate me and want to fight against me. When I'm tempted to worry and take matters into my own hands, I want to step back and let You be God. My trust is in You! Amen.

THE LORD WILL BE BETWEEN US

Jonathan said to David, "Go in peace. For we have promised each other in the name of the Lord, saying, 'The Lord will be between me and you, and between my children and your children forever.'"
1 SAMUEL 20:42

Father, I'm so thankful for the gift of friendship. Thank You for blessing me with friends. Even if I have just a few close friends, I'm thankful for the way they help me get through life. Could You please help me be a good friend? And would You please bring friends into my life who totally and completely love You? It would be amazing to have a friend who points me to You. I pray for forever friends too. Even if I have no idea who might end up being a part of my life for years and years, I pray that even now You'd make our friendship stronger. Amen.

FALLiNG DOWN iN WorSHiP

Then all of the angels standing around the throne and around the leaders and the four living beings got down on their faces before God and worshiped Him. They said, "Let it be so! May our God have worship and shining-greatness and wisdom and thanks and honor and power and strength forever. Let it be so!"

REVELATION 7:11–12

Lord, You alone are awesome and amazing! Nothing in this world can even compare to You. Because of Your greatness, You deserve praise forever and ever. When I read that the angels will fall down on their faces and worship You, I want to join them. I praise You! You are all-wise and all-powerful. Thank You for all You've done to save Your people and all You've done in my life. You are worthy of honor and praise forever and ever. Amen!

He Has Great Plans for You

O Lord, You are my God. I will praise You. I will give thanks to Your name. For You have been faithful to do great things, plans that You made long ago.

ISAIAH 25:1

O Lord, You are my God! I praise You! Thank You for choosing me to be Yours. Thank You for doing amazing things in my life. Even if I don't always remember or realize it, You have a plan and a purpose for my life. Long before I was born, You planned great things for me. That's mind-blowing! Because You have plans for me, I can trust You. I'm so thankful I don't have to muddle through this world all in my own strength or in my own wisdom. I'm so grateful I can turn to You and count on You. I love You!

Good News of Peace

*Then Christ came and preached the
Good News of peace to you who were
far away from God. And He preached
it to us who were near God.*

EPHESIANS 2:17

Lord Jesus, thank You for coming to earth to rescue people from being judged for our sins. Thank You for bringing Your Good News of peace. In fact, *You* are the Good News of peace! You didn't keep anyone away from Your Good News—You brought it to people who were far from God and close to God. It didn't matter if they were young or old, man or woman, rich or poor, sick or well. You've gladly offered Your rescue to absolutely anyone. Because of You, Your death, and Your life after death, I can be made alive in You. When I say that You are Lord and believe God the Father raised You from the dead, I'm saved and made alive in You. That's Good News!

FOLLOWING THE RULES

The Law of the Lord is perfect, giving new strength to the soul. The Law He has made known is sure, making the child-like wise.
PSALM 19:7

Lord, as much as I may not always be happy about needing to follow someone else's rules, instructions are a very good thing! As long as they're right and true, good instruction can lead me to a better life. I want to remember that Your law is a very good thing. In fact, it's perfect! Following Your rules will make me wiser. I can trust what You've told me to do and not to do. I need to make sure I read the Bible more and more so I know what You've said. Thank You for wanting to guide me to a better life instead of leaving me to try to figure things out on my own. Amen.

Beautiful!

How beautiful on the mountains are the feet of him who brings good news, who tells of peace and brings good news of happiness, who tells of saving power, and says to Zion, "Your God rules!"

ISAIAH 52:7

Lord God, I want to grow up to become a beautiful woman someday, but not like the world classifies beauty. Right now, it seems like there's so much importance on looks and what outward beauty is. But what a person looks like on the outside doesn't last. Fads change and people get old. What won't change is my inner beauty. If I can become beautiful on the inside, that will last until my dying day. Your Good News brings happiness and saving power that others don't have. When I tell other people about Your peace, I become more and more beautiful from my head all the way to my toes. Please help me become beautiful in this way! Amen.

Want Some More?

Then Jesus said to them all, "Watch yourselves! Keep from wanting all kinds of things you should not have. A man's life is not made up of things, even if he has many riches."

LUKE 12:15

Jesus, You know people get distracted by belongings very easily. It was true when You walked the earth, and it's true today. It's definitely true in my own life. I admit I can get so distracted by what I have and what I don't have. It's easy to want more or want something different, and it's easy to start obsessing over those wants. When I do that, I forget to be grateful for the things I actually do have. I forget to thank You for all You've given me. Please forgive me! I really am thankful for Your good gifts. I want to focus on those the next time I'm tempted to think greedy thoughts. Amen.

Rest on Every Side

So the nation of Jehoshaphat was at peace.
His God gave him rest on all sides.
2 CHRONICLES 20:30

Father, You have the power to save and protect me. Sadly, it's easy for me to fall into fear. I don't want to live my life being afraid of what could happen to me. I want to live boldly, knowing You will do what's best for me. When I believe that You're for me, I can live at peace. I have nothing to fear. I'll be the first to admit I don't know how to make everyone at peace with me. In fact, sometimes I disappoint or frustrate people by the things I say or do. Please work in my thoughts, words, and actions so I can be more of a peacemaker. In Your name I pray, amen.

WHO DO I HONOR?

They did know God, but they did not honor Him as God. They were not thankful to Him and thought only of foolish things. Their foolish minds became dark. They said that they were wise, but they showed how foolish they were. They gave honor to false gods that looked like people who can die and to birds and animals and snakes. This honor belongs to God Who can never die.
ROMANS 1:21–23

Father, so much in this world takes my attention away from You. Sometimes I'm easily distracted by these people or things and give them more importance than they deserve. In fact, sometimes I give more honor to things and ideas than I give You. I know You, but I don't always honor You as God. I'm so sorry! Please forgive me. I want to worship and honor You! Amen.

your UNFailiNg Love

May Your loving-kindness comfort me
because of Your promise to Your servant.
PSALM 119:76

Lord, I try to find comfort in a lot of things. Sometimes I head straight to food or shopping. Other times I look to my friends' approval. And still other times I try to find comfort by zoning out in front of a screen. None of those quick fixes actually bring lasting comfort though. They may cheer me up for a little while or seem to numb my thoughts and feelings. But true, I-can-feel-it-deep-down comfort is found in Your never-ending love. You've promised me a kind of love that will never let me go. Your love doesn't keep track of the times I let You down. It will remain forever and ever. I want Your love to comfort me when I feel sad, angry, or disappointed. I want Your love to fill up my heart and overflow into my thoughts, actions, and words. Amen.

WHat IS GOOD?

O man, He has told you what is good.
What does the Lord ask of you but to do
what is fair and to love kindness, and to
walk without pride with your God?
MICAH 6:8

Lord God, opinions change so quickly. It's hard to decide what I should or shouldn't do. Instead of deciding my opinions based on what other people tell me, I want to make my decisions because of what Your Word says I should do! I don't need to wonder what is good, and I don't need to wonder what You require of me. In every situation, I need to treat everyone fairly. I need to love kindness and seek it out. And I need to walk humbly with You. Thanks for telling me what is good! In Your name I pray, amen.

WHO SHOULD I PLEASE?

*Do you think I am trying to get the
favor of men, or of God? If I were
still trying to please men, I would
not be a servant owned by Christ.*

GALATIANS 1:10

Lord, it's so hard to not try to please people. If I
try hard enough or do what other people ask me
to do or look or act a certain way, I get praise. It's
nice to find favor with others! But before I jump
through everyone else's hoops, I need to slow
down and remember I don't have to be a people
pleaser. The One I really should focus on pleasing
is You. It doesn't matter what my friends think.
And my family's opinions don't matter as much
as Yours. To be Your servant, I need to please You.
No one else's approval really matters. Please
help me remember this and break my chains of
people-pleasing thinking. Amen.

BeiNg KiND to tHe Cruel

If the one who hates you is hungry,
feed him. If he is thirsty, give him water.
PROVERBS 25:21

Father, it's so hard to be kind to people who are cruel! I'd rather stay away from bullies. When people say mean things to me, I get so hurt and angry. When people go out of their way to do mean things to me or my friends, I want to get back at them. I get really upset when people pick on me or people I love. So when I read what Jesus taught about loving your enemies, I feel uncomfortable. And when Proverbs teaches to feed your enemy if he or she is hungry or give your enemy water if he or she is thirsty, I don't like it. But I know it's the right thing to do. Even if it's really tough, I still need to obey. Please help me!

CHoosiNG WHat'S HarD But RiGHt

Do that which makes you complete.
Be comforted. Work to get along
with others. Live in peace. The God
of love and peace will be with you.
2 CORINTHIANS 13:11

Lord, it's so hard to live in peace with people. Especially when someone has hurt my feelings, I would rather hold a grudge. But You don't ask me to do what would make me most comfortable. What I'm supposed to do, whether I'd like it or not, is to try to get along with everyone. I need to live in peace with my friends and my enemies. I need to try to create unity, even with people who don't agree with me. Father, I could whine and complain and tell You how much I really don't want to do this. Or, I could choose to obey You and watch the way You pour out Your love and peace in my life. Please help me trust You completely!

BrokenHearted

*The Lord is near to those who
have a broken heart. And He saves
those who are broken in spirit.*
PSALM 34:18

Father God, I absolutely hate the feeling of a broken heart. When I feel so sad and disappointed and helpless, it feels like my very spirit is crushed. Being heartbroken hurts. You never intended for humans to deal with feelings like this. Your creation was absolute perfection until sin entered the picture and dashed everything to pieces. Even if broken hearts weren't part of Your original plan, I still need to deal with those feelings. Please help me feel Your comfort when I'm upset. I want to pour out all my thoughts and feelings to You, so You can take the pieces of my heart and put them back together in a beautiful way. Thank You for staying close to me no matter what. Amen.

TAKING MY PUNISHMENT

But He was hurt for our wrong-doing.
He was crushed for our sins. He was
punished so we would have peace. He
was beaten so we would be healed.
ISAIAH 53:5

Lord Jesus, I don't deserve all You've done for me. You were hurt for the wrong things I've done. You were crushed for my sins. My punishment was given to You. You were beaten for me. So that I wouldn't have to suffer for my sins forever, You chose to bleed and die for me. I absolutely deserve the punishment for all I've done wrong. Yet You've willingly taken it—if only I ask You. I'm so sorry for Your sacrifice, yet so completely grateful. Thank You for stepping in so I could live forever. Thank You for bringing me peace and healing. You are so worthy of my praise! In Your name I pray, amen.

Strength in Weakness

I receive joy when I am weak. I receive joy when people talk against me and make it hard for me and try to hurt me and make trouble for me. I receive joy when all these things come to me because of Christ. For when I am weak, then I am strong.
2 CORINTHIANS 12:10

Lord, joy seems like it should be an impossibility in the middle of tough times. But with You, anything is possible! When I'm weak, You can bring me joy. When people talk against me, You can fill me with Your joy. When people try to stir up trouble, I don't have to worry or cower in fear. You can bring me joy! As long as I know and trust and love You, You'll fill me with Your joy and strength. Even when I feel totally weak and completely helpless, You'll make me strong. Thank You!

Truth Instead of Lies

The pains given by a friend are faithful,
but the kisses of one who hates you are false.

PROVERBS 27:6

Father, sometimes when my friends tell me the truth, it hurts. I'm not talking about their opinions, which could change. I'm talking about what I know is true. I may not want to hear it, but I need to listen. Please help me keep an open heart and mind to what they say. As hard as it is for them to tell me, when they tell me the truth in love, they're trying to help me. What I can't trust, though, is when enemies flatter me just to try to make me feel better or to win my affection. Please help me know the difference between the two. As nice as compliments make me feel, I don't want to get wrapped up in them. In Jesus' name I pray, amen.

UNEXPECTED KINDNESS

*"If the one who hates you is hungry,
feed him. If he is thirsty, give him water.
If you do that, you will be making
him more ashamed of himself."*

ROMANS 12:20

Lord God, it's so hard to be kind to my enemies! When they're mean to me, it's hard not to be mean in return. When they hurt my feelings, I want to hurt them too. When they insult me, I'd love to get revenge. But as Your daughter, You ask me to do things very differently than the rest of the world. You ask me to be kind to mean people. In fact, I should do nice things when people treat me badly. Please help me do what doesn't come naturally to me. Please help me be kind no matter what. In Jesus' name I pray, amen.

My Safe Place

For You have been a safe place for me,
a tower of strength where I am safe
from those who fight against me.

PSALM 61:3

Father, I don't always feel like I'm safe. When I feel like I'm in danger, I feel afraid. Other times I listen to what might happen and it scares me. Maybe some of the danger is very real and maybe some of it's imagined, but it leaves me wrestling with fear and doubt. Could You please help me? When I've trusted in You, You've been a safe place for me. It's easy to look around at what's happening and feel myself fill with fear. Please help me take a step back, focus on You, and worship You. You can wipe all my fears away when I trust You. Amen.

Right or Wrong?

"The Lord of All said, 'Do what is right and be kind and show loving-pity to one another.'"
ZECHARIAH 7:9

Lord, Your way of doing things is really, really good. In fact, it's so much better than anything I can choose on my own. But it's different from things I might feel comfortable doing. For instance, You've said I need to do what's right. I need to be loving and kind to other people. Those are all really good things, and I definitely want other people to be kind and forgiving to me. But to live it out every day? It's hard! Sometimes I like holding grudges. I get grumpy and don't feel like being kind to everyone. Other times, I'm tempted to do what's wrong. Even when I'm tempted to do my own thing, please help me choose to follow You and do what's right in Your eyes. Amen.

Choosing to Be Quiet

Be quiet and know that I am God.
I will be honored among the nations.
I will be honored in the earth.

PSALM 46:10

Father, when I think of everything happening in the world right now, it's easy to worry and be afraid. I could imagine what might happen and get really stressed out. Or, I could quiet my mind, be still, stop obsessing over what-ifs, and know that You are God. You're the Lord of all. You're above everything else, and nothing happens that You don't allow to happen. You're the One who will be honored among the nations and in the entire earth. I won't be honored. Other people alive today won't be honored. It's You and You alone. When I'm quiet and choose not to worry, I will remember this and know that You are God. In Your holy name I pray, amen.

Be My Light

Do not have joy over me, you who hate me. When I fall, I will rise. Even though I am in darkness, the Lord will be my light.
MICAH 7:8

O Lord, I know enemies are people created in Your image, just like me. But I don't like the way they treat me! I don't like how angry and hurt I feel when I deal with them! It seems like life would be better—or at least easier—without them. I need to remember that even if I don't like the way they make me feel, they can help me learn how not to treat people and how not to deal with problems. Even though it feels like I've fallen and can't get up, please help me rise and be stronger than ever. Even though it feels like I'm in the dark and can't see the right way to go, please light my way. Amen.

Work for Peace

*Work for the things that make peace and
help each other become stronger Christians.*

ROMANS 14:19

Father, peace doesn't come naturally. As much as I'd like to wish people could get along peacefully, disagreements usually bring the opposite result. Even if other people try to argue or pick a fight, I can work for the things that make peace. Please help me look past hurtful words and actions. Please help me be kind even when people disagree with me. Please help me forgive even if and when I don't feel like it. Could You please use my gentle responses and my attempts to be a peacemaker to help other people become stronger Christians? Give me the strength and patience to do this work, please! In Jesus' name I pray, amen.

Out of the Mud

He brought me up out of the hole of danger, out of the mud and clay. He set my feet on a rock, making my feet sure.
PSALM 40:2

Lord, sometimes it feels like I'm in the middle of a slimy pit here on earth. I feel like I'm slogging through really gross, really hard times. I can't seem to keep my footing very steady because I'm slipping and sliding and feel like I'm ready to fall on my face. But You have a way of pulling me out of this sloppy mess. You can lift me right out and set my feet on a firm rock. I can catch my breath and not worry about falling down. Thank You! Thanks for being my firm foundation. Thanks for being my steady, sturdy helper. I don't want to think of what my life would be like without You! Amen.

No Matter What

*"The mountains may be taken away
and the hills may shake, but My loving-
kindness will not be taken from you. And
My agreement of peace will not be shaken,"
says the Lord who has loving-pity on you.*
ISAIAH 54:10

O Lord, Your kindness for me is something I'll always be grateful for but never fully understand. No matter what happens in this world, I can trust You and Your never-ending love for me. Your favor will continue no matter what. Your promise of peace won't change, even when it seems like all peace disappears in this world. Even if and when natural disasters happen all around me, I still can trust You and Your goodness. If everything steady and reliable around me caves in, I still can trust in You. You're my Rock! Your faithful love and protection are such good gifts. Thank You! I love You!

FRIEND OF GOD

It happened as the Holy Writings said it would happen. They say, "Abraham put his trust in God and he became right with God." He was called the friend of God.
JAMES 2:23

Father, sometimes I wonder if I'm doing all I can to become right with You. If I work hard at trying to be good, will You love me more? If I disobey, will You turn against me? Instead of figuring things out on my own, Your Word has answers and examples to follow. Abraham was a man who was really important to You—he was the father of Your nation and was called Your friend. How did Abraham get all these blessings and favors? He put his trust in You. Even when it seemed like everything was against him, he kept trusting in You and Your promises. That faith made him right with You. I want to put my trust in You too! Amen.

DON'T BE SCARED!

"Have I not told you? Be strong and have strength of heart! Do not be afraid or lose faith. For the Lord your God is with you anywhere you go."

JOSHUA 1:9

Lord, I'm afraid! When I think about what might happen to me, I get scared. My fears are based on what-ifs though. What if something happens? What if my worst fears come true? Instead of fearing possibilities, I only need to focus on the reality of what's here and now. You haven't commanded me to be afraid. Instead, You've commanded me to be strong! And courageous! I don't have to live in fear. I don't have to be discouraged. What I need to remember is You're with me wherever I go. You're always with me! Knowing that the God of the universe is with me all the time to strengthen and guide me makes me feel brave. Thank You!

Freedom to Love

Christian brother, you were chosen to be free.
Be careful that you do not please your old
selves by sinning because you are free. Live
this free life by loving and helping others.
GALATIANS 5:13

Father, I'm so thankful You've called me to be free! So much in this world tries to enslave me, whether it's people telling me what to do or rules I need to follow. I feel like I'm always trapped, trying to figure out what rules I need to obey. You have Your own rules, but they bring me life instead of consequences. They bring me freedom instead of tying me down. Please help me use my freedom in You to serve in kindness instead of going crazy with sin and making myself happy. I'd love to make other people happy by helping them. Please help me serve others the way Jesus served. Amen.

Safe With Him

*For You are my rock and my safe
place. For the honor of Your name,
lead me and show me the way.*

PSALM 31:3

Lord God, You're my safe place! I can run to You
when I'm afraid and when it seems like my world
comes crashing in. You're strong and steady and
never changing, just like a rock. I'm so thankful I
can totally rely on You. Please lead me. In Your
perfect wisdom, please show me the way to go.
I want to do what You've planned for me, but I
don't know what it is! Could You please guide
me? Because I'm Yours, I know I don't have to
fear. I can get excited about the unknowns in my
future, because I know You're in control. What a
relief! Thank You for Your peace. In Jesus' name
I pray, amen.

Love and Kindness

I led them with ropes of human kindness, with ties of love. I lifted the load from their neck and went down to feed them.

HOSEA 11:4

Lord, when I read the Bible and see the ways You love and lead Your people, it makes me feel all warm and fuzzy. You led the Israelites with cords of human kindness and ties of love. This was completely kind and gentle. It wasn't like Your people were following You as slaves or by force. There's nothing harsh about the way You guide. You don't talk down to humans or treat us like we're unworthy to get Your care. You treat us just like we're made in Your image, and that makes me know how much I mean to You. You are a good, good God, and I love You!

A BUNCH OF BELONGINGS

*We came into this world with nothing.
For sure, when we die, we will take
nothing with us. If we have food
and clothing, let us be happy.*
1 TIMOTHY 6:7–8

Father, I admit I think about my belongings more than I probably should. I consider what clothes and shoes I want to wear. I have my favorite possessions that bring me comfort. I take a lot of time cleaning up my stuff because I have so much. And when I'm not focused on belongings or hobbies, I really like figuring out what to eat next. I like food! You've given me so much. Thank You! As much as I like these things, though, they won't last forever. Please help me focus more on how I'm loving You more and becoming a better me than on gathering a bunch of belongings. In Your name I pray, amen.

HeLP!

Listen to my prayer, O God. Do not hide Yourself from what I ask. Hear me and answer me. My thoughts trouble me and I have no peace, because of the voice of those who hate me and the power of the sinful. For they bring trouble upon me, and in anger they keep on having bad thoughts against me.

PSALM 55:1–3

Father, I'm so upset when people hate me. Their hate bubbles over in their words, attitudes, and threats. I don't know what to do! They're trying so hard to scare me just so I'll do what they want me to do, but I don't want to cave in. Their opinions aren't the only ones that matter in the world! Your way is the best way. I have my own thoughts, and I can make my own decisions. As long as I honor You, I don't want other people to sway me. Amen.

Peace Instead of Panic

*"Peace I leave with you. My peace
I give to you. I do not give peace to
you as the world gives. Do not let
your hearts be troubled or afraid."*

JOHN 14:27

Lord Jesus, You knew You couldn't stay on earth forever, but before You left You gave such a good gift to Your followers. You gave Your peace! Your peace is amazing. It's not like anything the world gives. You've given peace of mind and a peace I can feel deep inside. Your peace takes away my fear. With Your peace ruling my heart, I don't worry. It's really pretty amazing. When the world around me spins into panic at any possible danger, I can stay calm. It's such a relief that I don't need to be a drama queen. I can rest in Your peace, and that makes my life feel so much better than a life of panic. Thank You!

Rest and Wait

Rest in the Lord and be willing to wait for Him.
Do not trouble yourself when all goes well
with the one who carries out his sinful plans.
PSALM 37:7

Oh Lord, waiting seems so hard! I want things to happen right away. But You have a way of making me wait for Your right and perfect time. I don't have to rush things. Even when I feel like I could burst in anticipation, I want to choose to wait. It's hard for me to wait when I watch people around me getting the things I want. Those people seem to do whatever feels right, or they go after anything they want without considering You. Please help me keep my eyes on You and not on them, even if it's hard to see what they're doing and not feel jealous. Please help me wait for Your perfect timing! Amen.

GoiNg Out With Joy

"You will go out with joy, and be led out in peace. The mountains and the hills will break out into sounds of joy before you. And all the trees of the field will clap their hands."
ISAIAH 55:12

Lord, I like to imagine going out with joy and being led in peace. It sounds so happy to me. When I think about going places, I don't always go out with joy. In fact, sometimes I'm pretty grumpy. And when I think of You leading me in peace, I realize how different it is when I try to lead myself. When I follow my own logic and decisions, I'm filled with doubts and worries. Please help me follow Your guidance. When I do, even nature will celebrate. Even though it sounds a lot like a fairy tale, I'd love to see everything celebrating with me! In Your name I pray, amen.

THe ANtiDote to Worry

Do not worry. Learn to pray about everything. Give thanks to God as you ask Him for what you need.

PHILIPPIANS 4:6

Lord God, it's so easy to be tempted to worry! When I listen to what's happening in the world or wonder about what might happen in my future or to people I love, it's easy to start thinking about bad things that might happen. Why is it so easy to think about the worst possibilities? Because of You, though, I don't have to worry. If I'd just learn to pray about everything, You'd fill me with Your peace. Please help me learn to trust You completely. Once my trust and faith in You grows, I won't have a reason to worry. The more I pray, the more I'll trust You and the more my worries will disappear! In Jesus' name I pray, amen.

FiND THE GOOD WaY

The Lord says, "Stand by where the roads cross, and look. Ask for the old paths, where the good way is, and walk in it. And you will find rest for your souls. But they said, 'We will not walk in it.'"

JEREMIAH 6:16

Lord, there's so much noise in this world! It seems like so many different messages are shoved in my face. I want to find the good way! If Your good way offers rest for my soul, I want it, even if it's so different than anything the world offers. The Bible explains that Your good way can be found by looking and asking for it. Your good way is a lot like GPS in the way that it will guide me to the right destination. It will tell me the right way to go. That's exactly what I need! Amen.

HOW WILL YOU BE FOUND?

Dear friends, since you are waiting for these things to happen, do all you can to be found by Him in peace. Be clean and free from sin.

2 PETER 3:14

Lord Jesus, Your disciple Peter taught how Your followers should live: people who follow You need to be at peace with You and free from sin. Living without sin makes me nervous, because I know I mess up every single day. Sometimes I don't mean to make mistakes, but other times I completely know what I'm doing wrong and choose to do it anyway. Please forgive me! I want to live in a way that shows my love for You. I want to make You happy with the things I say and do. In Your name I pray, amen.

Your Guide to the End

This is God, our God forever and ever.
He will show us the way until death.

PSALM 48:14

Father, knowing You are God forever and ever makes me realize how awesome You are. You always have been God, You are God, and You always will be God. There's never been a split second in all eternity when You weren't God. I can't fully understand You or explain You, but I'm in awe of You! Knowing You'll willingly guide me is absolutely amazing. You'll be my guide until the end—until I take my last breath in this life. You're the Creator of all and Lord of heaven and earth. And You willingly guide me. Thank You! I don't want to get in Your way. Please help me trust and follow You. In Jesus' name I pray, amen.

No Need to Fear

"Be strong and have strength of heart. Do not be afraid or shake with fear because of them. For the Lord your God is the One Who goes with you. He will be faithful to you. He will not leave you alone."
DEUTERONOMY 31:6

Lord, it's easy to get distracted by people who don't like me. When I remember things they've said about me or done to me, I get so upset. I don't want them to keep invading my thoughts. I don't want to dread seeing or hearing them. And I don't want to live in fear. The great news is You go with me every single day everywhere I go. I'm never alone. Thank You for Your love and devotion and care! Because of You, I can be strong! I can be brave and full of courage. Because of You, I don't have to live in fear! Amen.

Being Sure

Now faith is being sure we will
get what we hope for. It is being
sure of what we cannot see.

HEBREWS 11:1

Father, when I think about what it means to have faith in something—or faith in You—I know it means that I have complete trust and belief in something I can't physically prove. I may not be able to see You right now. It's not like I can introduce You to my friends so we can all sit around and have a conversation with You. But I know You're there. You show Yourself in my life every single day! In some ways, You're like the wind. I may never be able to see the actual wind, but I can see the effects of the wind. I can hear and feel the wind. Just like I'm certain wind exists, I'm certain You exist too. I am sure of You! Amen.

Don't Be a Hater

Do not be full of joy when the one who hates you falls. Do not let your heart be glad when he trips.
PROVERBS 24:17

Father, You know I'm not always nice or kind. I may not always be really mean, but I take sides. I have favorite people. I know who I want to spend time with and who I'd rather avoid. I even have enemies. And I have a hard time forgiving people who make my life miserable. For those people who go out of their way to be mean to me, please help me see them through Your eyes. When they mess up and I'm tempted to celebrate, please stop me in my tracks. When they come into really hard times, please stop me from being glad. Even if I will never truly be their friend, please help me show way more kindness to them than I feel like I can. Amen.

Greatness and Honor

"Greatness and honor to our God in the highest heaven and peace on earth among men who please Him."

LUKE 2:14

Lord Jesus, when You were born, the angels came to announce Your birth with so much incredible joy and praise. As they celebrated Your birth, they honored God. They also wished peace to those people on earth who please God. If I choose to praise You and believe in You and trust You as my Lord and my God, Your favor rests on me. That's amazing! Even if I feel like my life is a teensy blip in the scope of eternity, it matters to You. When I please You, I get to experience true peace. I want Your love to inspire me to do big things for You. I want to celebrate You with incredible joy and praise, just like the angels! Amen.

His Song

The Lord will send His loving-kindness in
the day. And His song will be with me in
the night, a prayer to the God of my life.
PSALM 42:8

Lord God, the way You love and care for me is breathtakingly beautiful. I really can't understand just how much You love me. But by day You direct Your love for me in a million different ways. I don't even realize all the ways You're lovingly working things out for my best. You direct me with Your love. And at night when I feel so alone, You're right there with me, comforting me with Your song. Your song is with me all night long, and even if I couldn't name the tune or the words, my heart knows it completely. As my heart sings along, it's a prayer to You. In Jesus' name I pray, amen.

CrooKeD or StraigHT

*They know nothing about peace, and
there is nothing fair in their paths. Their
roads are not straight. Whoever walks
on them does not know peace.*

ISAIAH 59:8

Father, I could go down very different paths in
my life. One path is what You've planned for
me. It's filled with peace. Another path is what
I choose to do on my own. This path doesn't
always have the clearest direction. Eventually
it will get me somewhere, but it's a very different
destination than I intended. Yet another path
is what the world lays out before me. This path
winds around in crooked, twisting directions
and leads me to places of regret. As fun as the
world's path might seem, and as much as my
own path seems all about me, I'd really like to
feel at peace. Having You guide me on Your
perfect path of peace sounds pretty great to
me! Amen.

WHY Worry?

"Do not worry about tomorrow. Tomorrow will have its own worries. The troubles we have in a day are enough for one day."

MATTHEW 6:34

Lord, most days it seems like I could worry about so much! From things in my own life to problems my friends and family face, I have a lot of concerns. When I add in school and what's going on in my community and what might happen in the world, I end up thinking about worry after worry. Jesus taught that I shouldn't worry about tomorrow though. That means I don't need to worry about what might happen in the future. What I can spend time thinking and praying about is what's going on today. Please help me focus on what's going on here and now. Please help me trust You more and more. Amen.

Living With Honor

"My agreement with him [Levi] was one of life and peace, and I gave them to him, that he might honor Me with fear. So he honored Me with fear. My name filled him with fear and wonder. True teaching was in his mouth, and no wrong was found on his lips. He walked with Me in peace and was right and good. And he turned many from sin."

MALACHI 2:5–6

Father, I've learned that Levi lived a life that honored You with fear and wonder. He told the truth, did what was right and good, walked with You in peace, and turned other people away from sin. I can try to be like Levi. I'd love to honor You. I want to turn people away from sin and teach Your truth. I want to be honest and do what's right and good. I want to walk with You in peace. Amen.

Live Like I Believe

We know God's Son has come. He has given us the understanding to know Him Who is the true God. We are joined together with the true God through His Son, Jesus Christ. He is the true God and the life that lasts forever.

1 JOHN 5:20

Father, so many people in this world don't know what truth is. They wander around believing every little lie and end up wrestling so much doubt. But You've let me know Your truth. And when I believe Your truth about Jesus, You fill me with peace and certainty. Through Jesus, You give me life that lasts forever. When I believe in Him and believe You raised Him from the dead, You give me forever life with Yourself. I believe, Lord! Please help me live like it! Amen.

A Glad Heart

*And so my heart is glad. My soul is full of
joy. My body also will rest without fear.*
PSALM 16:9

Lord, because of You, my heart is glad. You fill
my soul with joy! When I see the way You work
in my life and I think of all You've done for me,
I'm so happy! I'm also relieved that I can fully
rest without any fear. Living with complete trust
in You and seeing the way You work wonderful
things in my life really fills me with joy. Thank
You for the way You're for me and not against
me. Thank You for the way You give me really
good gifts time after time. I want my love and joy
for You to shine in my life so others can come to
know You too. Please use my life to bring others
closer to You. In Your name I pray, amen.

SHOW ME!

Show me Your ways, O Lord. Teach me Your paths. Lead me in Your truth and teach me. For You are the God Who saves me. I wait for You all day long.

PSALM 25:4–5

God, my hope is in You all day long. From the time I wake up until the time I fall asleep, I'm so glad I can trust You completely. I admit that I get confused though. Please straighten out my thoughts so I don't have to feel all muddled. I want to follow You. Could You please show me Your ways? And could You please teach me Your paths? I have a hard time figuring it all out on my own. Guide me in Your truth, please. I want to read Your Word more and more so I know what Your truth is. When I do read the Bible, please teach me in the way only You can. Amen.

Scripture Index

OLD TESTAMENT

NEW TESTAMENT